Twenty Names In Medicine

Eleanor van Zandt

Illustrated by Gary Rees

MARSHALL CAVENDISH
New York, London, Toronto

Editor: Rosemary Ashley
Consultant Editor: Maggi McCormick

Reference Edition published 1988

Published by Marshall Cavendish Corporation
147 West Merrick Road
Freeport
Long Island
N.Y. 11520

Library of Congress Cataloging in Publication Data

Van Zandt, Eleanor.
Twenty names in medicine / Eleanor Van Zandt
p. cm. — (Twenty names)
Bibliography: p.
Includes index.
Summary: Presents brief biographies of twenty individuals who made significant contributions to medicine
ISBN 0-86307-963-6 : $12.95
1. Physicians-Biography-Juvenile literature. 2. Medicine-History-Juvenile literature. [1. Physicians, 2. Medicine-History.]
I. Title. II. Title: 20 names in medicine.
III. Series.
R134. V36 1988
610' .92'2-dc19
[B] 88-20998
[920] CIP
AC

Printed in Italy by G. Canale & C. S.p.A. - Turin.

Contents

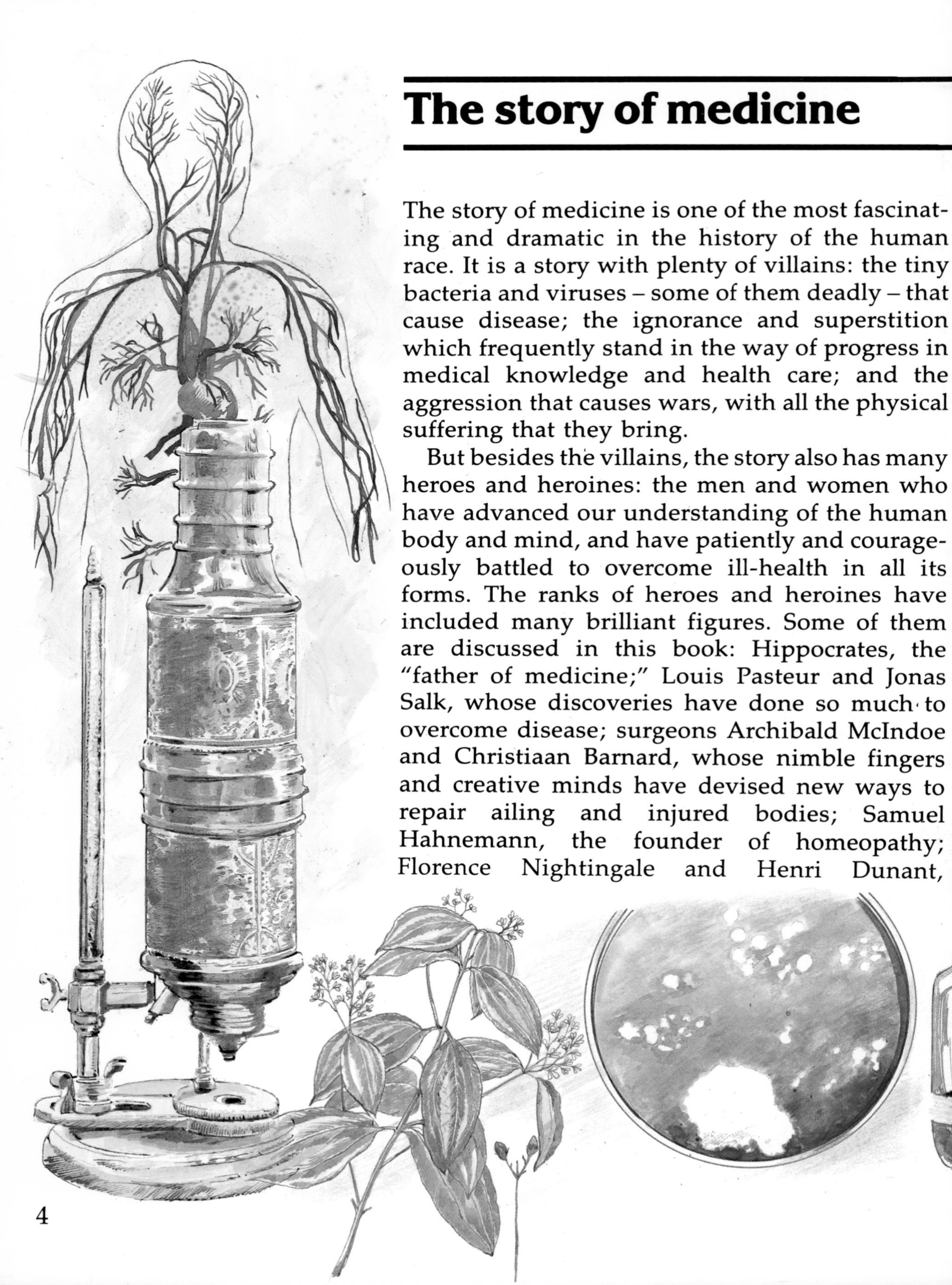

The story of medicine

The story of medicine is one of the most fascinating and dramatic in the history of the human race. It is a story with plenty of villains: the tiny bacteria and viruses – some of them deadly – that cause disease; the ignorance and superstition which frequently stand in the way of progress in medical knowledge and health care; and the aggression that causes wars, with all the physical suffering that they bring.

But besides the villains, the story also has many heroes and heroines: the men and women who have advanced our understanding of the human body and mind, and have patiently and courageously battled to overcome ill-health in all its forms. The ranks of heroes and heroines have included many brilliant figures. Some of them are discussed in this book: Hippocrates, the "father of medicine;" Louis Pasteur and Jonas Salk, whose discoveries have done so much to overcome disease; surgeons Archibald McIndoe and Christiaan Barnard, whose nimble fingers and creative minds have devised new ways to repair ailing and injured bodies; Samuel Hahnemann, the founder of homeopathy; Florence Nightingale and Henri Dunant, humanitarians who devoted their lives to the care of the sick and injured.

Throughout the ages, innumerable men and women – doctors, nurses, chemists, herbalists, pharmacists, midwives and many, many others – have contributed to the struggle for good health and the fight against disease. In this book, we include a few of them, some famous and others not so famous, who, with their different talents and personalities, have all contributed to the fascinating and dramatic story of medicine.

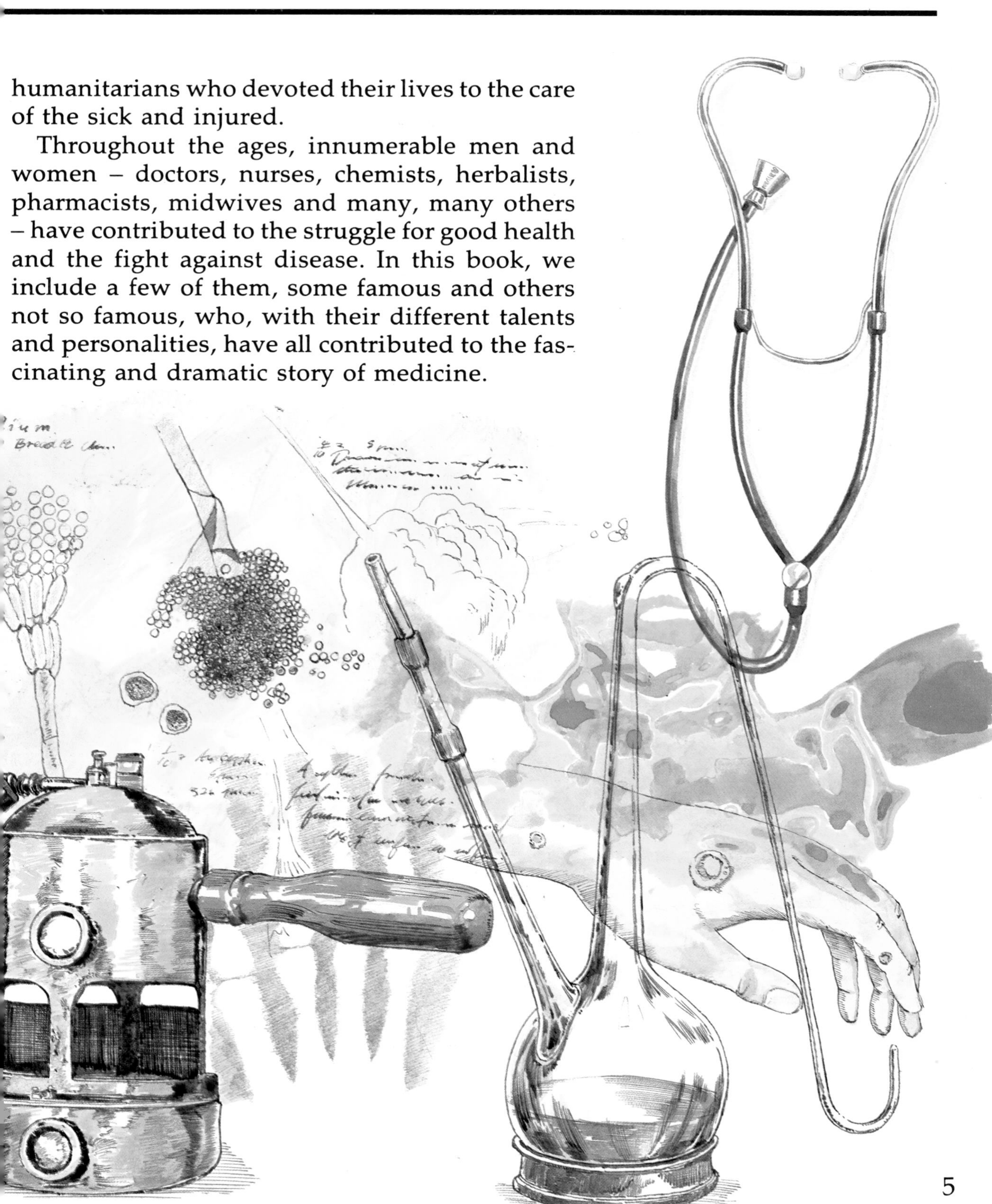

1

Hippocrates

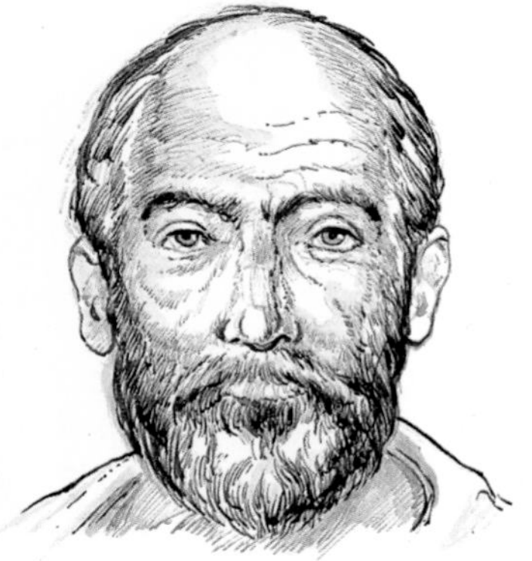

Little is known about the life of Hippocrates, but he was probably born in the fifth century BC, on the Greek island of Cos, into a family that had produced many well-known physicians. The treatment of illness in Ancient Greece was linked to worship of Aesculapius, the god of healing. Many patients probably benefited from the good care they received in the temples of Aesculapius, but their recovery was believed to be the result of divine intervention.

Hippocrates argued that illness was the result of natural causes – not supernatural ones – and that its treatment should be based on scientific principles. He made careful notes on the course of each disease and kept detailed records of individual patients' health. In this way, he gradually compiled a mass of information that could help

Hippocrates teaching his medical principles to students on the island of Cos.

him make accurate diagnoses and give suitable treatment. He understood that the body has its own healing mechanisms and recommended a healthy way of life as a means of preventing disease.

Hippocrates was revered not only as a physician, but also as a teacher. He taught in many places in Greece and other Mediterranean lands, but was most closely associated with the medical school on Cos. A collection of writings known as the "Hippocratic Collection" may have formed the library of this school, but we do not know which of these, if any, were written by Hippocrates himself.

One of these writings is the famous Hippocratic Oath, a code of ethics for doctors which is still used in the graduation ceremonies of some medical schools. Although it may not have been written by Hippocrates, the oath serves as a tribute to the man who put the treatment of illness on a scientific basis and who, for this reason, is known as the "father of medicine."

Part of the Hippocratic oath
. . . The regimen I adopt shall be for the benefit of my patients according to my ability and judgment, and not for their hurt or for any wrong. I will give no deadly drug to any, though it be asked of me, nor will I counsel such, and especially I will not aid a woman to procure abortion. Whatsoever house I enter, there will I go for the benefit of the sick, refraining from all wrongdoing or corruption . . . Whatsoever things I see or hear concerning the life of men, in my attendance on the sick or even apart therefrom, which ought not to be noised abroad, I will keep silence thereon, counting such things to be as sacred secrets.

2

Paracelsus

One of the most colorful characters in the history of medicine, Paracelsus delighted in shocking the established authorities, both in his native Switzerland and elsewhere. As a youth in the early sixteenth century, he wandered around Europe attending one university after another. He was not impressed with the standards at any of them except the University of Ferrara in Italy: here, medieval medical teachings were criticized. He claimed that he had received his doctor's degree from this university: "A doctor must seek out old wives, gypsies, sorcerers . . . and take lessons from them," he said.

His pursuit of knowledge led Paracelsus to many distant lands. From herbalists, he learned of the healing properties of plants; from alchemists, those of chemicals. In the course of his travels, he cured many sick people; and when

1493	Born in Einseiden, Switzerland (real name Philippus Aureolus Theophrastus Bombast Von Hohenheim
1510	Graduates from University of Vienna
1516	Receives doctor's degree from University of Ferrara, Italy
1527–8	Town physician and lecturer in medicine, University of Basle, Switzerland
1536	Publishes *Die grosse Wundartzney* ("The Great Surgery Book")
1541	Dies in Salzburg, Austria

he returned to Switzerland in 1524, he found that he was famous. The University of Basle appointed him to be lecturer in medicine.

This appointment lasted less than a year. Because Paracalsus attacked accepted medical practices, even setting fire to the approved texts, he made many enemies. Finally, he had to flee the city. Later, his writings and his cures revived his reputation. He was welcomed by royalty, and eventually his work brought him a lot of money.

Paracelsus made many contributions to medicine. He discovered the link between certain diseases and a person's environment or occupation – for example, between silicosis (a lung disease) and the particles inhaled by miners underground. He established the role of chemicals in treating disease. Perhaps most important of all, he inspired others to approach the study of medicine with open minds.

Above *A fifteenth-century woodcut of an apothecary's shop.*

Left *Paracelsus studied different methods on his travels, and he cured many sick people. He disagreed with established medical practice and caused the textbooks to be burned.*

3

Ambroise Paré

In the sixteenth century, when Ambroise Paré was born, surgery was not a highly respected profession. Most surgery, in fact, was carried out by barbers, as a sideline, and consisted mainly of tooth extractions, amputations and some other simple operations. The few physicians who practiced surgery were only slightly more knowledgeable than the barber-surgeons.

Paré had had little formal education when he went to Paris in his early twenties. However, he managed to secure a place as an apprentice in surgery at the Hôtel-Dieu, a famous hospital in the city. There, he acquired enough knowledge of anatomy and surgery to qualify for a post as a surgeon in the French army.

The horrors of war provided Paré with plenty of surgical experience, and his open-minded

1510	Born in Bourg-Hersent, France
c 1533	Begins apprenticeship at Hôtel-Dieu, Paris
1537	Becomes army surgeon
1545	Publishes his book "The Method of Treating Wounds Made by Harquebuses and Other Guns" (translation)
1552	Is appointed surgeon to King Henry II
1590	Dies in Paris

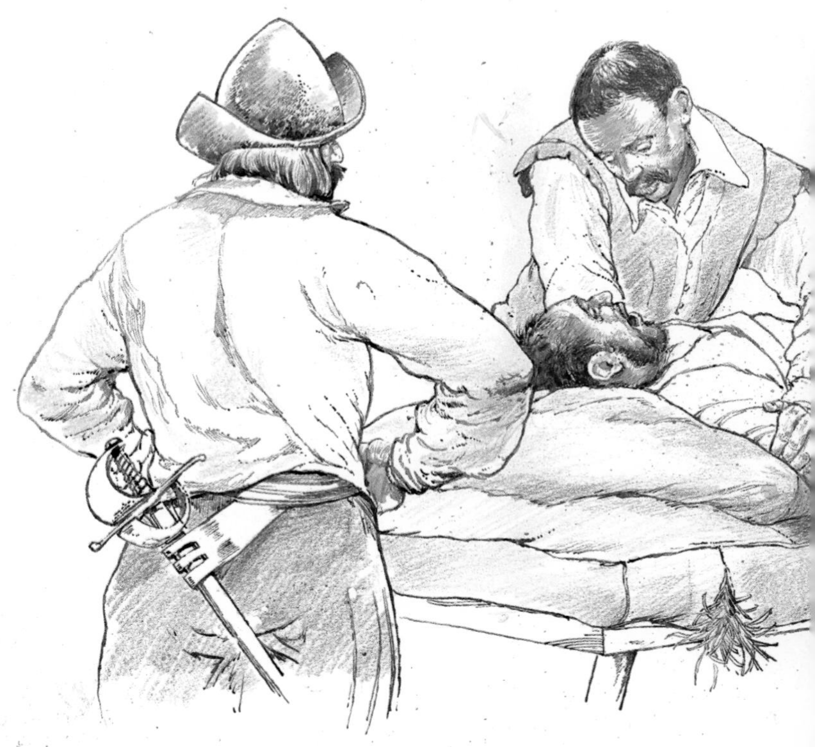

attitude led him to make several improvements in accepted surgical technique. He discovered that gunshot wounds healed much more readily when treated with a mild dressing rather than with the standard treatment, which consisted of bathing the injured part with boiling oil. To reduce loss of blood during amputations, he tied the large arteries, rather than searing them with hot irons, as was the usual practice.

Paré's reports of his discoveries were ridiculed by the medical establishment of the time because he wrote in French instead of Latin. "The work of a very impudent and ignorant fellow," said one. But his skill and his sensible approach won his patients' admiration and gratitude. After leaving army service, he became surgeon to four successive kings of France.

During his long career, Paré invented many scientific instruments and devised new surgical methods. Because he set new, high standards for his profession, he is often called "the father of modern surgery."

Above *A surgeon examines a patient in the fifteenth century.*

Left *Paré learned his surgical skills treating soldiers injured on the battlefield.*

4

Andreas Vesalius

Even as a boy in Brussels, Andreas Vesalius was fascinated by the structure of bodies. He would cut open dead mice, birds and other small animals and examine the bones, muscles and organs.

Later, as a medical student, he had the opportunity to study human corpses. But the dissections performed in the lecture halls were crudely carried out by assistants, while the professors taught anatomy according to the writings of Galen, a physician of Ancient Rome. Galen's description of the human body was based mainly on that of the Barbary ape – human dissections were forbidden in those days – but his word on anatomical discoveries was considered sacred.

Vesalius continued his studies at the University of Padua, in Italy, Europe's foremost medical school, and was then made professor of surgery

1514	Born in Brussels (Flemish name Andries Van Wesel)
1529–37	Studies medicine at universities of Louvain, in Brabant (Belgium), at Paris and at Padua (Italy)
1537	Receives Doctor of Medicine degree from Padua and is made professor of surgery and anatomy
1543	Publishes the *Fabrica*; is appointed court physician to Emperor Charles V
1559	Is appointed court physician to King Philip II of Spain
1564	Dies on the Greek island of Zacynthus

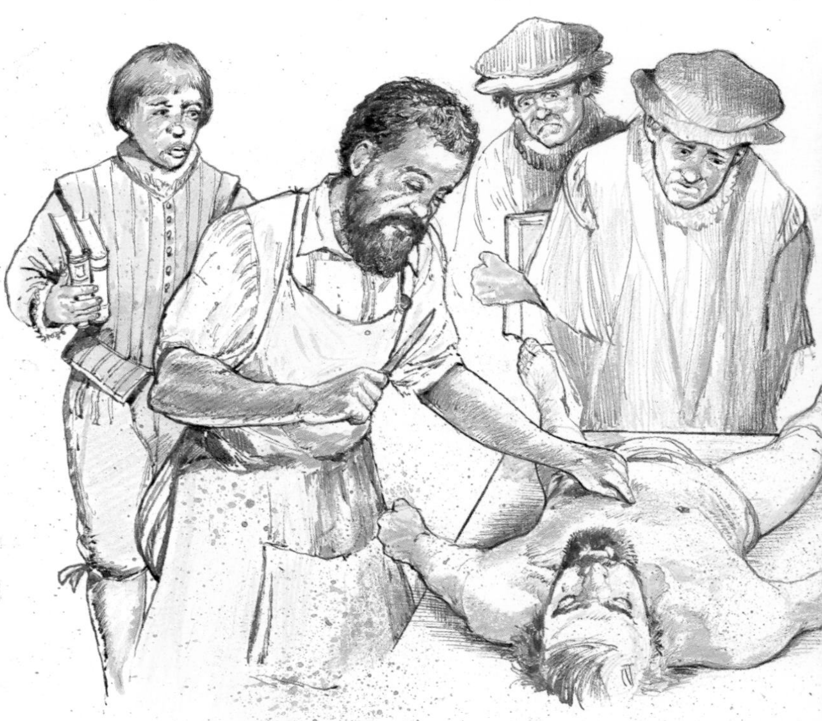

and anatomy. Students came from all over Europe to hear Vesalius lecture. As he talked, he dissected the corpse himself. When he could not see the connection between Galen's anatomy and the evidence before him, he declared that Galen was wrong.

In the meantime, Vesalius was writing his masterpiece. *De Humani Corporis Fabrica Libri Septum* ("Seven Books on the Structure of the Human Body") was the first complete book on human anatomy. Based on his own obervations, it contained a wealth of new, accurate information, and was illustrated with many beautiful drawings.

Although controversial, the *Fabrica* did not damage Vesalius' reputation: he was appointed court physician to the Holy Roman Emperor Charles V. Wealth, prestige, even a title came his way before he died, at the age of fifty, while on a pilgrimage to the Holy Land.

Above *An illustration from the* Fabrica *showing Vesalius demonstrating his anatomical findings.*

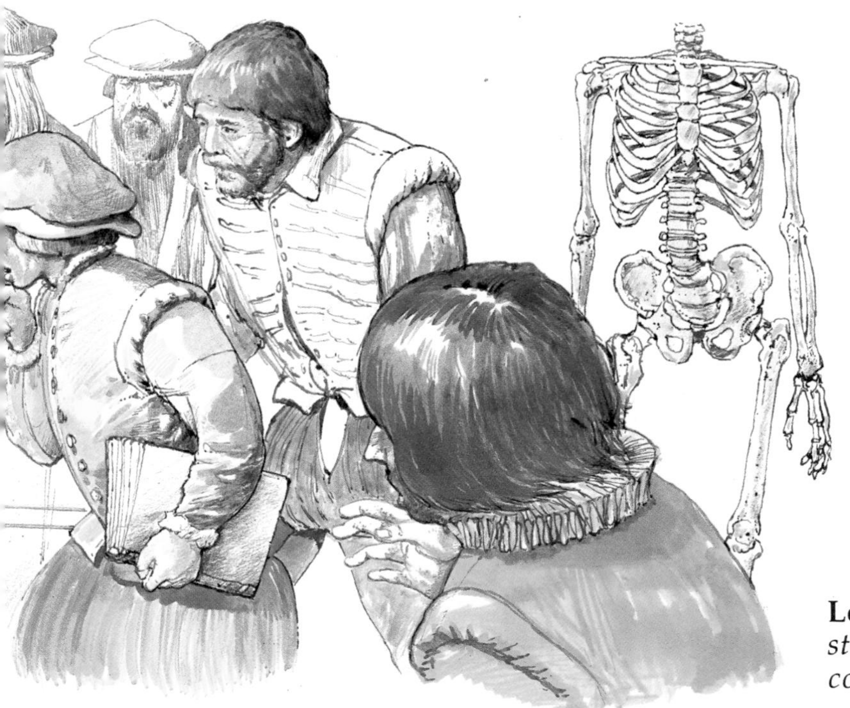

Left *Vesalius lecturing to students while dissecting a corpse.*

5

William Harvey

Before the year 1628, it was generally believed that blood ebbed and flowed in the body, rather like the motion of the sea. The veins, with their dark red blood, and the arteries, carrying bright red blood, were thought to be separate systems.

These theories were beginning to be questioned when a young graduate from Cambridge University in England, William Harvey, came to the University of Padua for advanced study in medicine. His anatomy professor, Hieronymous Fabricius had discovered that the veins contain tiny membranes which he called valves. However, Fabricius did not know what purpose these valves served.

After returning to England, Harvey settled in London. He became a fellow of the College of Physicians, obtained a post at St. Bartholomew's hospital, and was appointed physician to King James I. At the same time, he pursued his research into the movement of the blood.

1578	Born in Folkestone, England
1597	Receives BA degree from Cambridge University
1602	Receives MD degree from University of Padua, Italy
1607	Becomes fellow of the College of Physicians
1609	Appointed to the staff of St. Bartholomew's Hospital, London
1618	Appointed physician extraordinary to King James I and later to King Charles I
1628	Publishes *De Motu Cordis*
1645	Appointed warden of Merton College, Oxford
1657	Dies, probably at Roehampton, near London

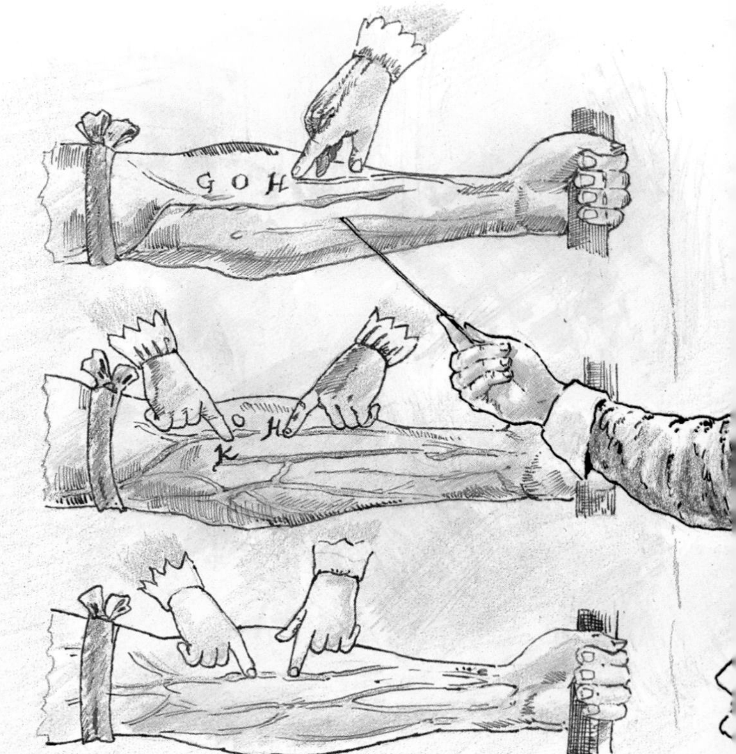

Finally, after countless observations, dissections and experiments, he published a small book entitled *De Motu Cordis et Sanguinis in Animalibus* ("On the Motion of the Heart and Blood in Animals"). Among other things, this book revealed that the heart is a pump, sending blood first through the lungs, where it exchanges carbon dioxide for oxygen, and then through the arteries (the main blood vessels) to all parts of the body. It also explained how the blood travels back to the heart through the veins, helped along by the valves. (The microscopes of that time were not powerful enough to show the tiny vessels, called capillaries, that we now know link the veins and arteries.)

Predictably, *De Motu Cordis* was widely attacked by the medical establishment of the time. Today, however, Harvey's discovery of the circulation of the blood is recognized as one of the most important advances in the history of medicine.

Above *Using the corpse of a dog, Harvey shows students how blood courses through the body.*

Below *Harvey demonstrating his discovery of the circulation of the blood.*

6

Edward Jenner

Less than two hundred years ago, smallpox was one of the most feared of all diseases. Frequent epidemics swept through Europe and America, killing thousands of people. Those who survived an attack could be scarred for life, or even blinded.

Today, smallpox has been virtually wiped out, largely thanks to an English country surgeon named Edward Jenner.

While still in his teens, Jenner had been apprenticed to a local surgeon. Then, he had studied in London under John Hunter, a prominent surgeon with a wide-ranging knowledge of biology. With Hunter's guidance, Jenner developed his natural talent for observation and experiment.

It was well known that a person who had survived smallpox was protected against (immune)

1749	Born at Berkeley, in Gloucestershire, England
1770–73	Studies under John Hunter in London
1796	Successfully vaccinates against smallpox
1798	Publishes *An Inquiry into the Causes and Effects of the Variolae Vaccinae*, the results of his experiments
1802 and 1804	Awarded funds totalling £30,000 by Parliament for work in furthering vaccination
1815	Retires from public life
1823	Dies at Berkeley

Below *Jenner inoculates' James Phipps with material taken from a smallpox pustule.*

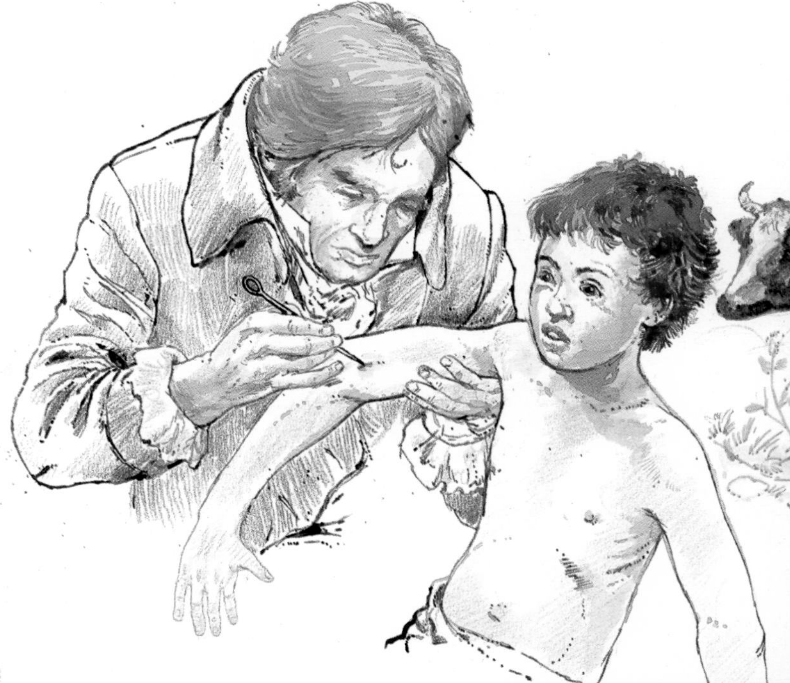

to any further attack. And in the countryside, where Jenner lived, it was also known that anyone who had caught cowpox, a skin disease common to cattle, would also become immune. Jenner wondered if this mild disease could be deliberately transmitted from one person to another to produce immunity to smallpox.

Jenner performed a bold experiment. He inoculated an eight-year-old boy, James Phipps, with material taken from a sore on the hand of a dairymaid who had cowpox. The boy became slightly ill, but recovered quickly. A few weeks later, Jenner inoculated James with matter taken from a smallpox pustule (spot). The boy remained well.

After making some more tests, Jenner published his results. At first, people were reluctant to try vaccination, as the method was called (after the Latin *vacca,* meaning "cow"), but, within a few years, the idea had caught on, and doctors in many countries were vaccinating people. The death rate from smallpox dropped dramatically. Jenner's experiment had begun one of medicine's greatest success stories.

Above *After Jenner's successful experiment, many people came to him for vaccination.*

7

Samuel Hahnemann

When Samuel Hahnemann began practicing medicine in Germany in the eighteenth century, there were few effective drugs available to prescribe. Patients were given vile-tasting concoctions which rarely improved their condition. Purging, induced vomiting and bloodletting (draining out blood) were favorite treatments for all sorts of illnesses.

The lack of good medicines frustrated Hahnemann in his work. Then, one day, while reading about the treatment of the tropical disease malaria by quinine – one of the few effective known drugs – he decided to take a little quinine himself, to see how it would affect a healthy person. He was surprised to note that it produced symptoms similar to those of malaria, except for the fever.

Could it be that "like would cure like," as some physicians in the past, including Hippocrates, had suggested? Hahnemann put the theory to the

Hahnemann records the effects on his body of taking quinine.

test. Over the following years, he tested many different substances. He gave small amounts to healthy volunteers and made detailed notes of their reactions. Then, when patients showed symptoms matching the effects of a particular substance, he would give them a tiny amount of it. The results were encouraging.

When a typhoid epidemic swept through the town of Leipzig in 1813, Hahnemann treated 180 patients with his new method, which he called "homeopathy" (after Greek words meaning "similar" and "disease"). Only one patient died.

This dramatic success brought fame to Hahnemann. But he was not popular in Leipzig, where his use of only tiny amounts of medicines which he mixed himself angered the apothecaries. After years of trying to practice his new form of medicine in different towns in Germany, where he met with much prejudice, he eventually settled in Paris. There, he was consulted by many doctors eager to learn more about the new system of medicine.

Today, although homeopathy is still regarded with doubt by many doctors, it is now a recognized branch of the medical profession.

1755	Born in Meissen, Germany
1770s	Studies medicine at Univerity of Vienna
1786	Becomes chief surgeon in Dresden
1796	Begins experimental work with medicinal substances
1810	Publishes *Materia Medica*, containing the results of his experiments
1813	Uses homeopathy successfully in typhoid epidemic
1815	Becomes lecturer in medicine, University of Leipzig
1821	Driven out of Leipzig because of unpopularity of his medical practices – moves to Cöthen
1843	Dies in Paris

8

Mary Seacole

During the Crimean War (1854–56), while Florence Nightingale and her nurses were working in the army hospital at Scutari, in Turkey (see overleaf), another remarkable woman was doing similar work, at Balaklava, on the Crimean peninsula, in southern Russia.

Born Mary Jane Grant, she was the daughter of a Scottish army officer and a black Jamaican woman. Her mother, a nurse, was skilled in traditional West Indian medicine. Mary was to follow in her footsteps.

Married briefly to a Mr Seacole, Mary was widowed while still young. For a while, she ran a hotel; then her love of travel took her to Central America. In the course of her travels, she learned more about healing, especially the treatment of tropical diseases.

When the British government appealed for nurses to care for the wounded in the Crimea,

Below *Mary Seacole distributes hot drinks among the troops embarking for the battle front.*

1805	Born in Kingston, Jamaica
1850	Helps in cholera epidemic, Kingston
1851–3	Travels in Central America
1854	Goes to London, then to Crimea
1857	Returns to London
1858	Publishes *Wonderful Adventures of Mrs Seacole in Many Lands*
1881	Dies in London

Mary Seacole sailed to England and volunteered her services. However, her offer was turned down.

Undaunted, she set off for the Crimea by herself. With the help of a distant relative, she opened the British Hotel in Balaklava, which quickly became known as a place where soldiers could get nourishing food and relax in comfortable surroundings.

Even before her hotel opened, however, Mary Seacole was at work among the troops, taking food, hot tea and medicines where they were needed, and giving first aid to the wounded. At her hotel, she successfully treated many cases of dysentery and other diseases. "Mother" Seacole, as the men called her, was loved and venerated.

After the war ended, Mary Seacole returned to England. She was seriously in debt. But the soldiers and officers remembered her and raised a fund for her. She wrote her memoirs and became a respected figure in London, where she spent most of her old age.

Above *A photograph of the army camp and harbor at Balaklava during the Crimean War (1854–56).*

9

Florence Nightingale

When Florence Nightingale was a girl, nursing was not the respected profession it is today. Hospitals were squalid places where poor people went to die, and most nurses were ignorant; untrained and often drunk. Florence's parents were horrified by her decision to become a nurse.

In spite of their opposition, Florence managed to attend a new school for nurses in Germany. Then, at the age of thirty-three, she became superintendent of a hospital for "sick gentlewomen" in London. Here, she showed a rare talent for organization and a great capacity for hard work.

In 1854, Britain declared war on Russia, and troops were sent to the Crimean peninsular on the Black Sea. When reports arrived from the battlefront describing the terrible conditions in the army hospitals, Florence was quick to respond. With thirty-eight other nurses under her charge, she set off for Scutari, in Turkey. There, she found

Below *Florence Nightingale worked ceaselessly, caring for the wounded in the hospital at Scutari.*

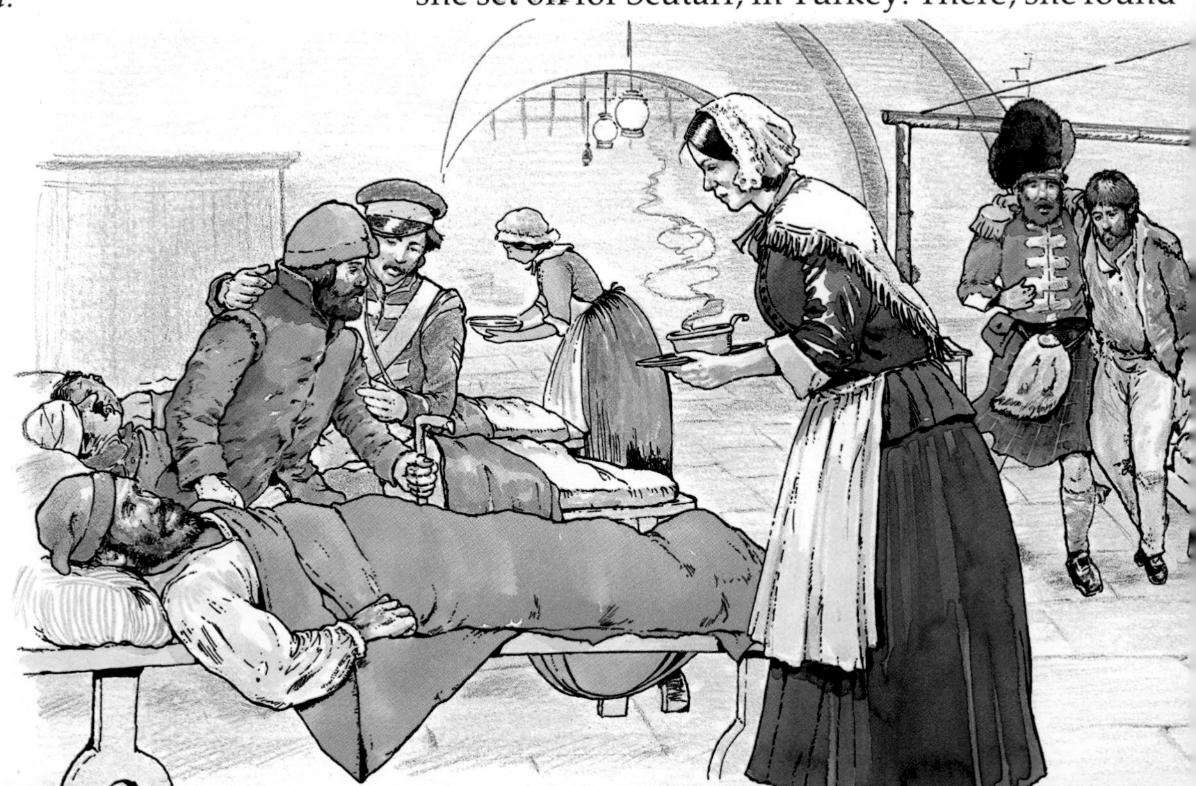

the makeshift hospital crammed with soldiers dying of their wounds, and of diseases spread by the filthy surroundings.

Florence soon had the wards cleaned, set up a laundry, and improved the food. She persuaded the authorities to install proper sanitation, which reduced the death rate from disease. Some of the doctors resented her interference, but the soldiers loved the "Lady with the Lamp," who walked through the wards every night, bringing them comfort.

Florence returned from the war a national heroine. A fund of £45,000 enabled her to establish the Nightingale School for Nurses at St. Thomas's Hospital in London. The high standards set there inspired the founding of similar schools in Britain and other countries.

For the rest of her life, Florence Nightingale worked tirelessly to improve hospital care.

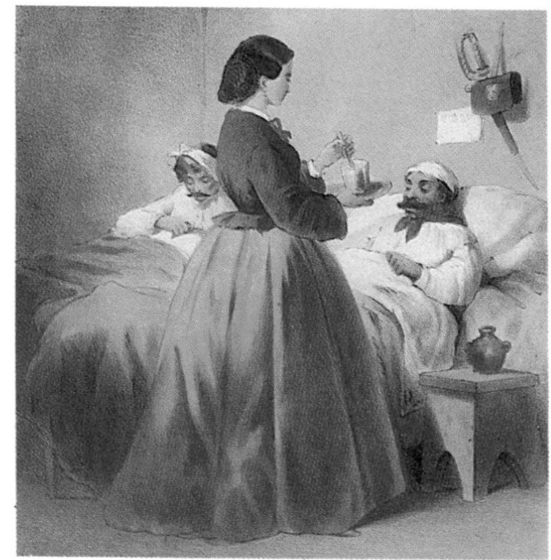

Above *Florence Nightingale's experiences at Scutari led her to establish nursing as the honorable profession it is today.*

1820	Born in Florence, Italy
1850	Trains as a nurse in Germany
1853	Becomes superintendent of the Institution for the Care of Sick Gentlewomen, London
1854–6	Works in the military hospital, Scutari
1859	*Notes on Hospitals* and *Notes on Nursing* published
1860	Nightingale Training School for nurses is opened
1901	Forced to give up work because of failing eyesight
1907	Receives Order of Merit
1910	Dies in London

10

Elizabeth Blackwell

It is not surprising that Elizabeth Blackwell had a strong social conscience. Her parents were people of liberal views; and, after the family moved from England to the United States in 1832, they became involved in the fight against slavery. Mr. Blackwell also made sure that his daughters, as well as his sons, had a good education.

In those days, there were no women doctors. So when Elizabeth decided that she wanted to practice medicine, she found the doors of the medical schools closed to her. But she continued to study medical books on her own, and finally she was admitted to a small medical school in New York State. Her dedication won the respect of the male students, and she graduated first in her class.

For practical training, Elizabeth went to Europe. After a course in midwifery in Paris, she

Below *Elizabeth Blackwell in the wards at the New York Infirmary for Women and Children, which she founded in 1857.*

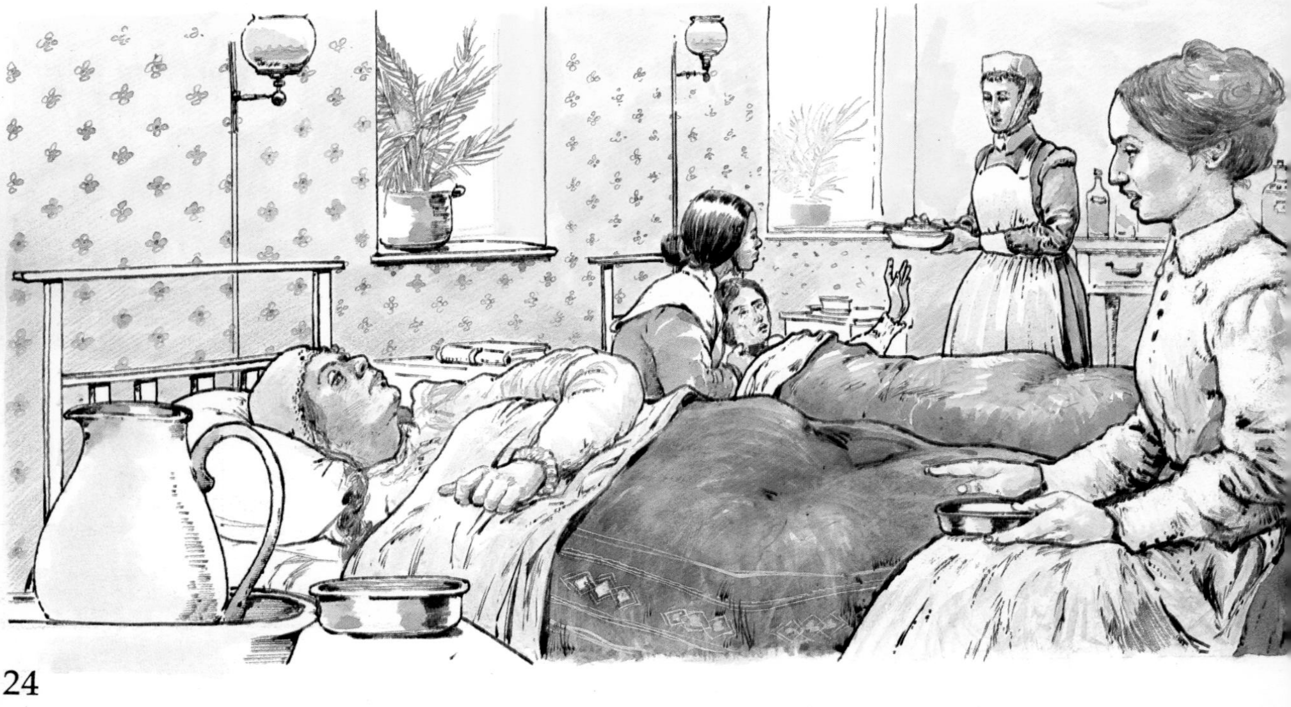

was given special permission to do further practical work at St. Bartholomew's Hospital in London.

Returning to the United States, Dr Blackwell slowly built up a practice in New York City. She also opened a dispensary in the slums, where she provided free health care for the poor. With the help of generous friends, she then opened the New York Infirmary for Women and Children. A few years later, the Infirmary became a medical school for women. At the same time, other American medical schools were starting to admit women students.

With the fight in America now won, Dr Blackwell returned to England. There, she joined her younger colleagues Elizabeth Garrett Anderson and Sophia Jex-Blake in founding the London School of Medicine for Women. By the time she died in 1910, the right of women to study and practice medicine was firmly established.

Above *Poor and sick New Yorkers line up for medicines at a dispensary in the city in the late nineteenth century.*

1821	Born in Bristol, England
1832	Moves to the US
1849	Graduates from Geneva Medical College, New York
1850	Studies at La Maternité, Paris, and St. Bartholomew's Hospital, London
1857	Opens New York Infirmary for Women and Children, New York
1868	The Infirmary becomes a medical school
1874	Helps to found the London School of Medicine for Women
1910	Dies in Hastings, England

11

Louis Pasteur

1822	Born in Dôle, France
1847	Receives doctor of philosophy degree from the Ecole Normale Supérieure, Paris
1848	Appointed professor of chemistry, University of Strasbourg
1853	Awarded Legion of Honor, France's highest honor
1854	Appointed dean of science faculty, University of Lille
1857–67	Becomes director of scientific studies, Ecole Normale Supérieure
1873	Elected to the Academy of Medicine
1882	Elected to the Academie Française
1895	Dies in Paris

Relatively few people have actually seen a germ, but we all know that they exist and that some of them cause disease. Louis Pasteur, the brilliant French chemist and microbiologist, succeeded in proving this fact. His accomplishments are among the most important of all scientific discoveries.

By the age of twenty-five, Pasteur had obtained his doctor's degree in science; at twenty-nine, he was a professor of chemistry at the University of Strasbourg. Higher university posts soon followed.

Pasteur became famous for his research into fermentation in food and alcohol. He discovered that this process was caused by microorganisms within the substance. Then, he developed a method of preventing undesirable fermentation by killing the microorganisms with heat. Called pasteurization, this process is used today to kill germs in milk and some other foods.

He also discovered other germs which caused diseases. He found the germ that caused a disease affecting silkworms and developed a means of preventing it – thereby saving the ailing French silk industry. And, by adapting Jenner's vaccination method, Pasteur was able to protect farm animals from certain serious diseases.

Then, in 1885, after three years of work, Pasteur produced a vaccine against the terrible and fatal disease, rabies. He tried the vaccine on a nine-year-old boy, Joseph Meister, who had been bitten by a rabid dog. The vaccine worked and the boy survived. Since then, thousands of people throughout the world have been inoculated with the vaccine and have been saved from developing rabies after being exposed to the disease. But the fight against rabies is not won yet. Lifetime immunity still cannot be provided, and treatment of the disease has not yet been perfected. However, research continues at the Pasteur Institute in Paris. Founded in 1888, it was headed by Pasteur himself until he died.

Above *Pasteur discovered ways of protecting animals and chickens from anthrax and chicken cholera.*

Left *Louis Pasteur at work in his laboratory.*

12

Joseph Lister

By the mid-nineteenth century, the use of anesthetics meant that surgery was no longer a terrifying experience for the patient. It was still, however, a dangerous experience: after an operation, the patient was very likely to die from infection.

Joseph Lister, an English surgeon at the Glasgow Royal Infirmary, noted that the death rate from infection among amputation cases was nearly 50 percent. Lister was familiar with Pasteur's work on fermentation, and he wondered if microorganisms similar to those that caused food to go bad might cause infection in wounds. Pasteur had shown that certain chemicals, called antiseptics, would kill microorganisms.

Lister decided to try a strong chemical called carbolic acid. He required his surgeons to wash their hands and instruments in a carbolic acid solution before operating. A dressing soaked

Right *An operation is carried out using Lister's antiseptic methods. A nurse operates an acid spray to kill germs.*

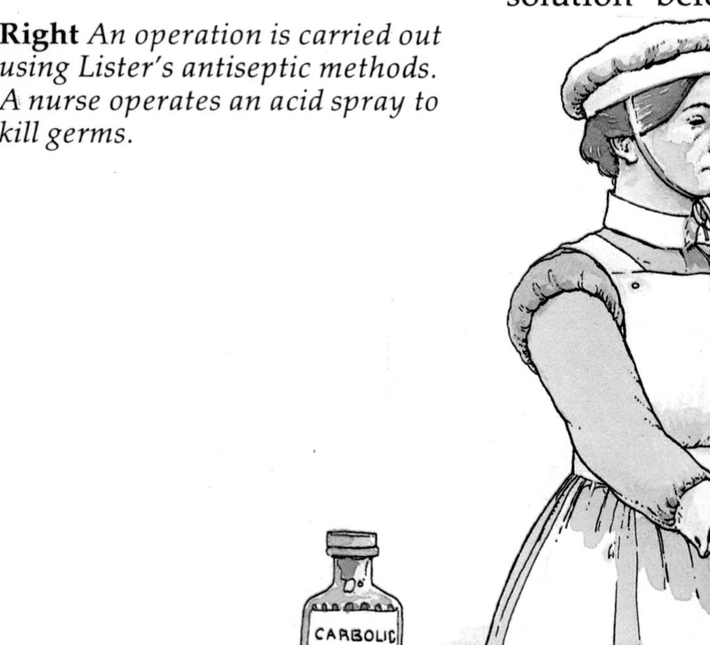

with the acid was applied to the open wound. Later on, Lister devised a method of spraying a fine mist of the acid through the operating theatre during the operation. There was immediately a sharp drop in the death rate following operations.

Only gradually, however, did surgeons elsewhere accept Lister's theory and adopt his methods. When they finally did, their results proved that he was right.

In his old age, Lord Lister, as he became, had the satisfaction of seeing his discovery almost universally accepted. By then, his methods had been developed even further: in place of antiseptic measures – to kill germs – surgeons had begun to use asepsis – to prevent germs from entering the operating theatre in the first place. In surroundings completely free from infection, they could now perform complicated life-saving operations that would have been unthinkable in the past.

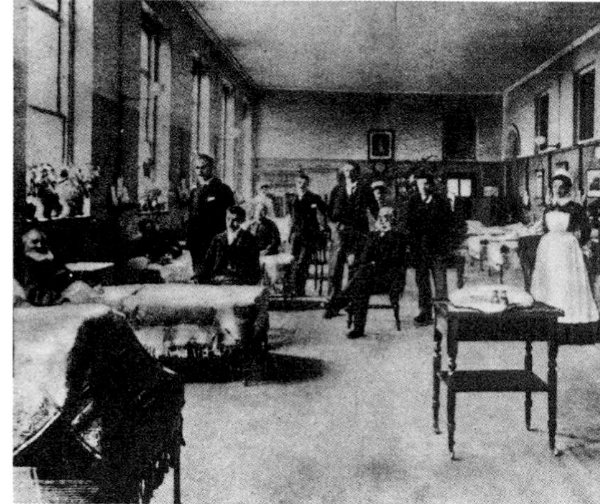

Above *Lister on a ward visit at King's College Hospital in London in 1891.*

1827	Born in Essex, England
1852	Receives bachelor of medicine degree, with honors, from University College, London
1856	Appointed surgeon to the Edinburgh Royal Infirmary
1861	Appointed surgeon to the Glasgow Royal Infirmary
1867	Publishes "On the Antiseptic Principle in the Practice of Surgery" in *The Lancet*
1877	Appointed professor of surgery at King's College Hospital, London
1897	Given the title of Baron Lister of Lyme Regis
1902	Awarded the Order of Merit
1912	Dies in Walmer, Kent

13

Henri Dunant

Henri Dunant was neither a doctor nor a scientist; he was a Swiss businessman. But he founded an organization that has been responsible for saving many lives: the Red Cross.

While traveling in Italy on business in June, 1859, Dunant saw the aftermath of the Battle of Solferino. This battle, fought between Austria and a combined French and Sardinian army, resulted in 42,000 casualties. Dunant was appalled by the plight of the thousands of wounded, left to die with no one to help them. So he took matters into his own hands. For three days, he worked on the battlefield, assisted by local people, tending the wounded of both sides.

Later, Dunant described his experiences in a book entitled *Un Souvenir de Solférino* ("A Memory of Solferino"). In the book, which he sent to influential people throughout Europe, he urged that all countries should set up voluntary organizations to relieve suffering in war. Then, he joined with four other citizens of Geneva to form a committee to promote this cause. It later became the International Committee of the Red Cross. In 1864, representatives of sixteen governments met in Geneva to agree on a set of rules, called the Geneva Convention, for the treatment of wounded soldiers. Soon, national Red Cross societies began to be formed.

Dunant had worked so hard to establish the Red Cross that he neglected his business; and by, 1867, all his money had gone. He spent the rest of his life in poverty, devoting himself to other good causes. In 1901, he was awarded the first Nobel Peace Prize.

The organization he founded now helps all kinds of people worldwide: not only the victims of war, but also those of accidents and natural disasters, the elderly and the handicapped.

Above *Red Cross ambulances transport the wounded in South Africa during the Boer War of 1899–1902.*

Below *Dunant worked on the battlefield at Solferino, caring for the wounded of both sides.*

1829	Born in Geneva, Switzerland
1855	Helps to found International Young Men's Christian Association (YMCA)
1859	Witnesses results of Battle of Solferino
1862	Publishes *Un Souvenir de Solférino*
1864	Red Cross founded
1867	Leaves Geneva, bankrupt
1901	Is awarded Nobel Peace Prize
1910	Dies in Heiden, Switzerland

14

Wilhelm Konrad Röntgen

1845	Born in Lennep in Prussia (Germany)
1869	Receives PhD from University of Zurich, Switzerland
1876–9	Professor of physics at University of Strasbourg
1879–88	Professor of physics at University of Giessen
1888	Becomes professor of physics at University of Würzburg
1895	Publishes "On a New Kind of Ray"
1900	Becomes professor of physics at Univeristy of Munich
1901	Awarded Nobel Prize for Physics
1923	Dies in Munich

As a boy in Germany, Röntgen was not a particularly good student, and at the age of sixteen he was expelled from school for his bad behavior. However, he managed to resume his education and, eventually, to obtain a PhD in physics from the University of Zurich.

Röntgen had been working for nearly thirty years as a university professor and experimental physicist when he made his great discovery. One evening he was working alone in his laboratory, passing an electric current through a glass tube to study the effects of cathode rays. On a nearby table was a piece of paper coated with a substance used in photography called barium platinocyanide. Röntgen noticed that, every time he passed the current through the tube, the paper gave off a greenish glow. This happened even when he placed a thick book between the tube and the paper.

For several weeks, Röntgen studied the mysterious invisible rays. He found that they would pass through some substances, but not through others. For example, the bones of his hand were

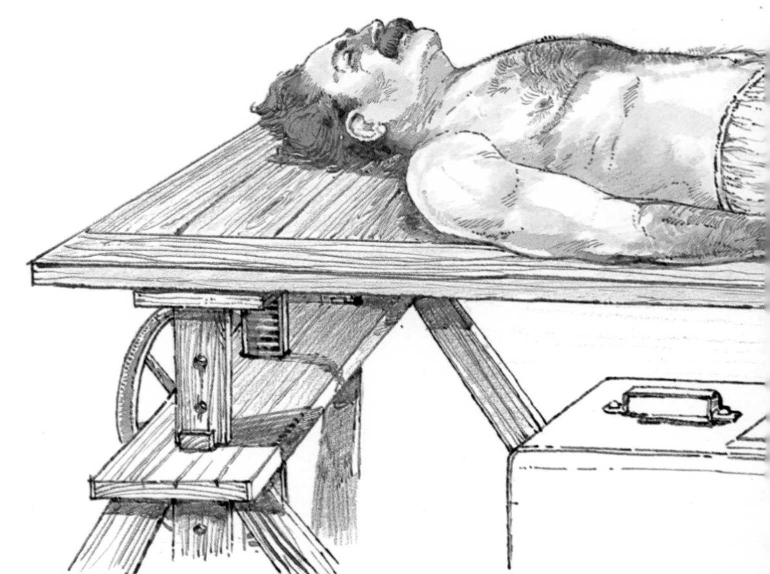

clearly outlined, because they blocked the rays. He also discovered that such images could be recorded on photographic plates.

Röntgen's discoveries, which he reported in a paper entitled "On a New Kind of Ray," caused great excitement in the medical world. Doctors and surgeons realized that these "X-rays," as Röntgen called them, could be useful in diagnosing and treating illness.

Few of them, however, could have guessed just how valuable these X-rays would prove to be. Today, ways of using and refining Röntgen's basic method are constantly being developed. For example, with the help of special dyes, X-rays can reveal organs and other body tissues in sharp detail, so that any defect can be identified and treated early. Many of the triumphs of modern surgery have been made possible by Röntgen's discovery.

Above *Doctors soon realized that Röntgen's discovery of X-rays could help greatly with diagnosis and treatment of illness.*

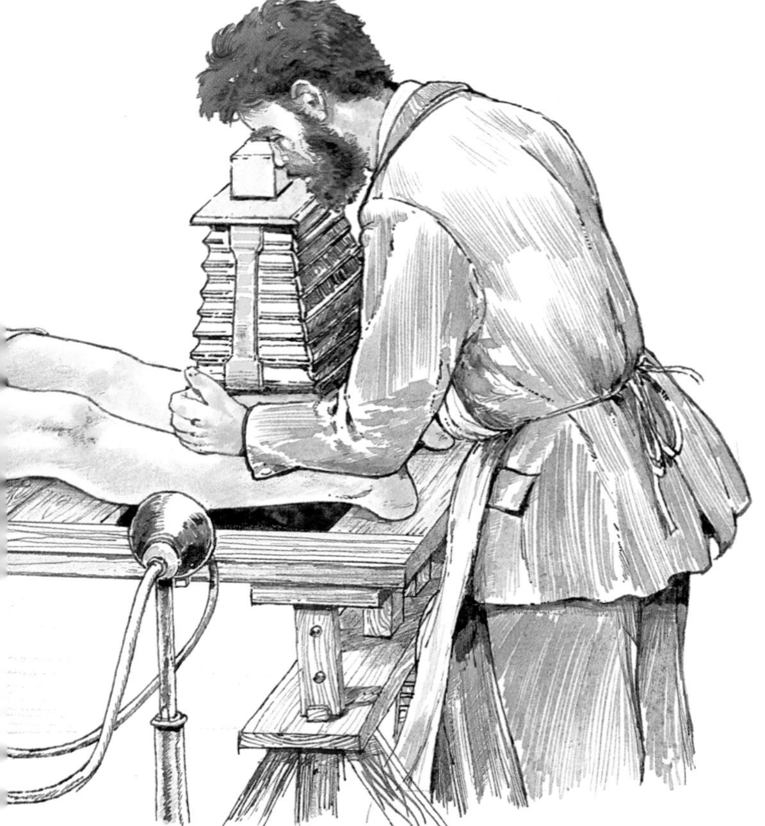

Left *Röntgen using his X-ray machine to study the bones in a patient's foot.*

15

Sigmund Freud

If we know more today than our ancestors did about the workings of the human mind, it is partly because of the findings of a brilliant Viennese physician named Sigmund Freud.

As a student, he found it difficult to decide on a career. He was interested in the work of Darwin and other scientists and also in philosophy. He finally chose medicine, and after studying in Paris, he started to practice as a neurologist in Vienna in 1886. As a young doctor, Freud became interested in the work of a colleague, Josef Breuer. One of Breuer's patients, a young woman called Anna, suffered from several puzzling symptoms, including paralysis, which came and went mysteriously. Breuer discovered that the symptoms would disappear under hypnosis, or even if Anna were allowed simply to describe her state of mind.

Freud tried Breuer's methods in similar cases, with some success. Gradually, over the years, he developed his own treatment, which he called psychoanalysis. In this treatment, the patient would lie on a couch and tell Freud anything that

1856	Born in Freiberg in Czechoslovakia
1859	His family move to Vienna
1881	Receives doctor of medicine degree from University of Vienna
1882	Begins work with Josef Breuer
1885	Studies hypnosis under Jean Charcot in Paris
1892	Begins developing psychoanalysis
1899	Publishes *The Interpretation of Dreams*
1902	Founds the Psychological Wednesday Circle, a group of early psychoanalysts
1938	Flees Vienna after Nazi takeover
1939	Dies in London

came into his or her head, no matter how silly or trivial it might seem to be. This process, called "free association," occasionally brought to the surface painful thoughts or childhood experiences that the patient had forgotten.

According to Freud, these thoughts and memories had been buried in an unconscious part of the patient's mind, emerging in the form of illness. In his book, *The Interpretation of Dreams*, Freud showed how these forbidden thoughts also appear, in disguise, while we sleep.

Many other doctors came to Vienna to learn about psychoanalysis from Freud. Later, some of them disagreed with some of his ideas, such as his emphasis on the role of sexual feelings in influencing a person's behavior. But the basic methods of psychoanalysis are still widely practiced today, and the importance of Freud's pioneering work is universally recognized.

Above *Freud writing up notes from his researches.*

Left *Freud's early experiments with psychoanalysis proved successful in treating certain illnesses.*

16

Alexander Fleming

Among the most effective drugs that a doctor can prescribe are the antibiotics. Their name comes from two Greek words meaning "against" and "life," and the "life" they attack is that of harmful bacteria which invade the body, causing illness.

The first antibiotic was discovered in 1928 by a Scottish bacteriologist called Alexander Fleming. At that time, Fleming was working at St. Mary's Hospital in London, studying a particularly infective type of bacteria, the staphylococcus bacteria. He had experimented by growing cultures of these bacteria in the usual way, on a jelly-like substance in flat glass dishes. One day, he noticed that one of the cultures had become contaminated: a green mold, similar to that which grows on stale bread, had started growing on it.

For Fleming's purposes, that culture was now useless. But, when he took a closer look, he found that, around the mold the bacteria had

1881	Born in Lochfield, Ayr, Scotland
1906	Receives degree in bacteriology from St. Mary's Hospital Medical School, London
1914–18	Serves in Royal Army Medical Corps during First World War
1918	Returns to St. Mary's to teach and conduct research
1928	Discovers penicillin
1943	Elected a fellow of the Royal Society
1944	Receives a knighthood
1945	Awarded Nobel Prize for Medicine
1955	Dies in London

disappeared. Obviously, the mold was producing something that killed the bacteria.

Having identified the mold as *Penicillium notatum,* Fleming went on to isolate its bacteria-killing substance, which he called penicillin. He found that penicillin was effective against certain bacteria even when diluted 800 times, and he correctly guessed that it could be useful to treat some diseases. But he was unable to work out a technique for its production on a large scale.

This breakthrough was achieved by two other scientists, Howard Florey and Ernst Chain, who managed, in 1940, to produce penicillin in quantity and test it. The results were encouraging. During the following years, rapid progress was made in developing penicillin. The substance has had a dramatic effect on health care in the twentieth century, and its widespread use has virtually eliminated many potentially deadly infections.

Alexander Fleming, along with Florey and Chain, was awarded the Nobel Prize for his work on penicillin.

Above *Fleming (center) discusses his findings with an Italian and a Russian colleague in Rome in 1945.*

Left *Fleming tests cultures of bacteria in his laboratory at St. Mary's Hospital, London.*

17

Archibald McIndoe

Many people think of plastic surgery in terms of removing wrinkles or giving someone a nicer-looking nose. But for the members of the Guinea Pig Club – men of the Royal Air Force who were badly burned when their planes were shot down during the Second World War – plastic surgery was a long and painful journey back to a normal life.

Among the surgeons who performed the delicate operations to rebuild the airmens' hands and faces was a formidable New Zealander called Archibald McIndoe. McIndoe was originally an abdominal surgeon, but he moved into plastic surgery soon after arriving in Britain in 1931. By the time war began in 1939, he had achieved a high reputation in this relatively new field and had been appointed head of the plastic surgery unit of the Royal Air Force at East Grinstead in Sussex, England.

1900	Born in Dunedin, New Zealand
1923	Graduates from Medical School of Otago University, New Zealand
1925–31	Studies and practices surgery at the Mayo Clinic, Rochester, New York
1931	Moves to England
1938–45	Appointed consultant plastic surgeon to Royal Air Force at Queen Victoria Hospital, Sussex
1942	Guinea Pig Club is formed, with McIndoe elected President
1947	Receives knighthood
1960	Dies in London

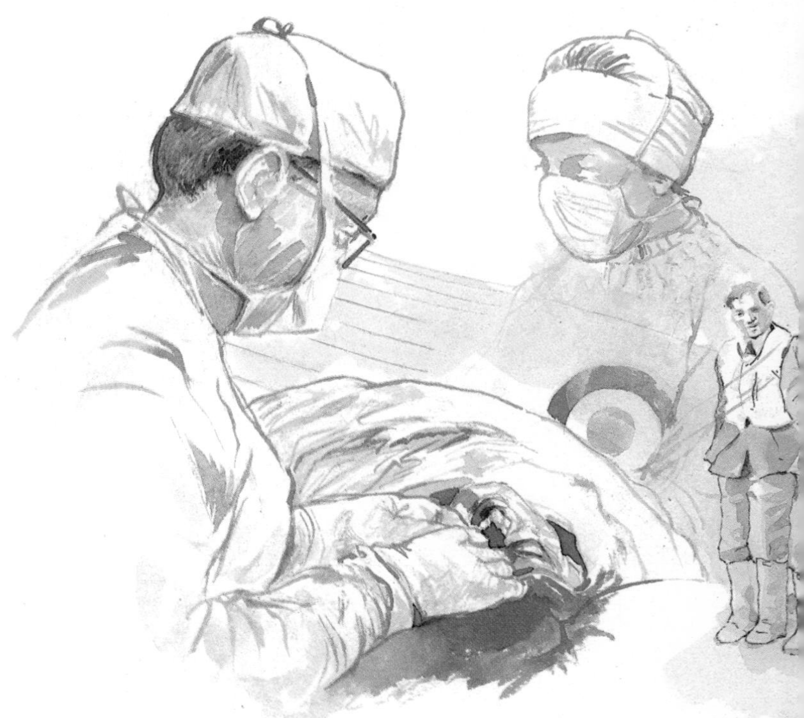

In 1940, as the Battle of Britain began, the patients started arriving. They looked like refugees from hell. Flames had destroyed noses, lips, cheeks, eyelids, and had stripped hands down to the bone.

Each case was different. Each required the artistic vision of a sculptor and the ingenuity of an inventor. McIndoe spent many hours planning how he would reconstruct each man's features, devising ways to solve new problems, not in the textbooks. For some of his patients, thirty or forty skin-grafting operations were necessary.

Over the months and years they spent in hospital, McIndoe's "guinea pigs," as the airmen called themselves, developed a great affection for their surgeon. Not only had he restored their faces: by encouraging them to get out into the world and not feel sorry for themselves, he had helped to restore their self-confidence.

Above *A "dog fight" during the Battle of Britain. Many of the pilots who flew the aircraft became McIndoe's "guinea pigs."*

Below *McIndoe's operations on badly burned airmen meant that many could return to a normal life.*

18

Mother Teresa

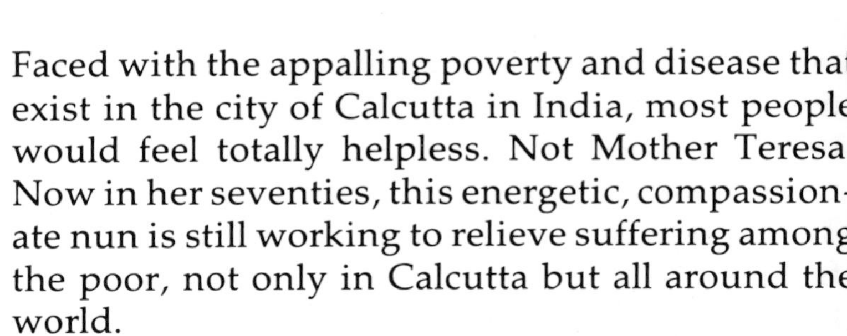

Faced with the appalling poverty and disease that exist in the city of Calcutta in India, most people would feel totally helpless. Not Mother Teresa. Now in her seventies, this energetic, compassionate nun is still working to relieve suffering among the poor, not only in Calcutta but all around the world.

Born in a part of Albania which is now in Yugoslavia, Agnes Gouxha Bejaxhiu (as she was christened) was still in her teens when she first went to India as a nun, having taken the name Sister Teresa. For twenty years, she taught in a convent school in Calcutta, eventually becoming its Mother Superior. But she became increasingly distressed by the squalor outside the convent walls; and, in 1948, she left her relatively comfortable convent life to study nursing and then to live and work among the poor.

Before long, Mother Teresa was joined by other women; and, in 1950, she founded her own order, the Missionaries of Charity.

1910	Born in Skopje (now Yugoslavia)
1928	Goes to Ireland to enter the Institute of the Blessed Virgin Mary, then to India
1928–48	Teaches at St. Mary's High School, Calcutta
1950	Founds Congregation of the Missionaries of Charity
1965	Work of the Missionaries of Charity begins outside India, in Venezuela
1979	Receives the Nobel Peace Prize

From simple beginnings – running a little school and distributing food and medicines where they were most needed – the Order's work has expanded enormously. In Calcutta alone, there are sixty centers, caring for the blind, the elderly, the crippled and abandoned children. Thousands of destitute people have been saved from death, and others have been taken into her home for the dying, where they are able to spend their last hours in peace and dignity.

Outside Calcutta, Mother Teresa has established a clinic and a village for lepers. Leprosy afflicts millions of people in India, and those who have this highly infectious and disfiguring disease are social outcasts. At the clinic and at special dispensaries elsewhere in India, thousands of lepers have been treated.

In 1979, Mother Teresa was awarded the Nobel Peace Prize in recognition of her work for poor, sick and oppressed people. Today, the order founded by Mother Teresa numbers more than 1,000 nuns, who have dedicated themselves to the care of the poor and the sick in many countries.

Above *Mother Teresa visiting children rescued from the famine in Ethiopia in 1984.*

Below *Mother Teresa distributes rice to starving people in Calcutta.*

19
Jonas Salk

Not so long ago, poliomyelitis was a greatly feared disease. Children were particularly likely to be affected, and although many suffered only a mild case of polio, some were left paralyzed. Others had trouble breathing and had to spend long periods of time in an iron lung. Some died.

It was in the United States, where a long and severe epidemic started in 1942, that the fight against polio was finally won.

The man who accomplished this feat was Dr. Jonas Salk. He had been an outstanding student, graduating from university when he was only nineteen years old. After completing his medical training, he decided to carry out medical research. His special interest was viruses – extremely tiny microorganisms that cause disease.

Salk began to study polio viruses in the late 1940s. There are a hundred different polio viruses, and it took Salk and his staff three years to classify

Below *Salk's research into viruses produced the first effective vaccine against polio.*

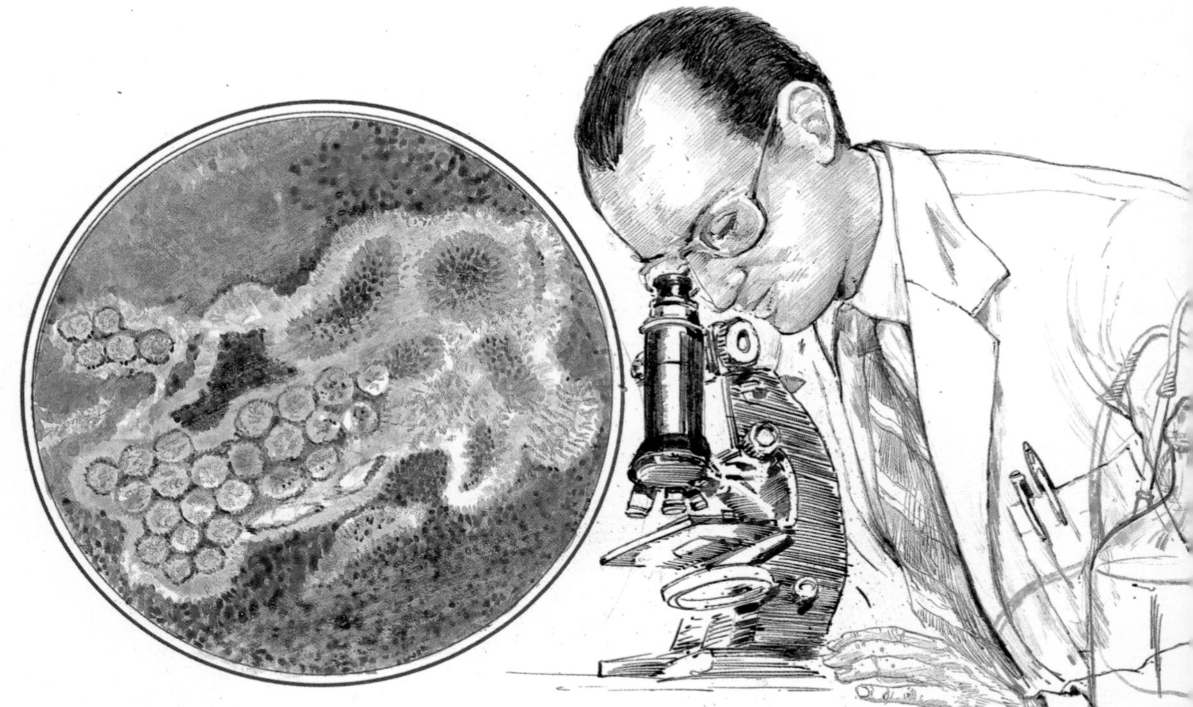

seventy-four of them. His research (along with similar work carried out at several other universities) proved that all of the strains fall into three main types, each of which attacks the central nervous system of humans in a different way. A polio vaccine would therefore need to contain viruses which had been inactivated in some way (treated to prevent activity) of all three types.

More painstaking work was required to develop the vaccine. The viruses had to be grown in the laboratory – no easy task. Many different mixtures were tried and tested, adjusted and combined, before Salk made a vaccine that could safely be tried on humans.

In 1953, the vaccine was tested on 1,000 children and adults in Pittsburgh. Follow-up examinations showed that the vaccine had stimulated the growth of antibodies (substances in the blood stream)that would give immunity to polio. Later, widespread vaccinations brought a sharp reduction in the number of serious cases of the disease. By the end of the 1950s, polio had been brought under control.

Above *Salk holds up bottles containing the culture used to grow the polio vaccine.*

1914	Born in New York City
1939	Receives MD from New York University College of Medicine
1947	Becomes head of Virus Research Laboratory, University of Pittsburgh
1949	Begins classification of polio virus strains
1955	Salk vaccine released for use in the United States
1963	Becomes director of Institute for Biological Studies (now Salk Institute) in San Diego
1977	Is awarded Presidential Medal of Freedom

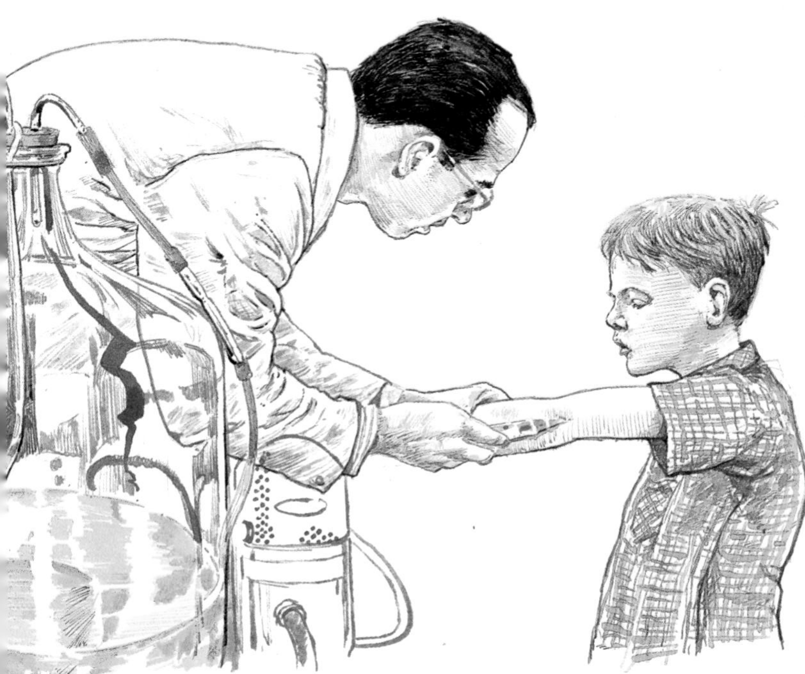

20

Christiaan Barnard

1922	Born in Beaufort West, South Africa
1953	Receives Bachelor of Medicine and Bachelor of Science degrees from University of Cape Town
1953–6	Resident surgeon at Groote Schuur Hospital, Cape Town
1958	Receives PhD in surgery from University of Minnesota
1958–83	Head of cardiac unit at Groote Schuur Hospital
1966	Does work in kidney transplants at Medical College of Virginia
1967	Performs first human heart transplant at Groote Schuur Hospital
1983	Retires from surgical practice

Modern surgery has provided many "miracles," but none has aroused so much excitement as the heart transplant. Even today, heart transplants often make news headlines; and the first transplant, performed in 1967, made the surgeon, Christiaan Barnard, world-famous.

Barnard grew up in rural South Africa, then studied medicine at the University of Cape Town. After several years as a surgeon in Cape Town, he went to the United States in 1956 for further study at the University of Minnesota. Surgeons there had developed an improved version of the newly-invented heart-lung bypass machine. This complex apparatus took over the tasks of pumping and oxygenating the blood, so that the heart, drained of blood, could be operated on.

At Minnesota, Barnard gained valuable experience in this new "open heart" surgery. Returning to South Africa in 1958, he set up that country's first open-heart surgery unit. He refined the

bypass machine and performed new surgery on the blood vessels and valves of the heart.

In 1967, Barnard and a team of twenty surgeons removed the heart of a young woman killed in a road accident and implanted it in the body of a fifty-five-year-old man, Louis Washkansky. The operation itself was a success, and Washkansky seemed on the way to recovery. But, within a few weeks, he died of pneumonia. Drugs given to him to prevent his body from rejecting the new heart had also lowered his resistance to disease.

Not long after this disappointment, Barnard performed another transplant. This time, the operation was successful, and the patient recovered. More transplants followed, and many of them were successful.

Barnard has now retired. But other surgeons in many countries now carry out heart transplants. Although the operation is still difficult and dangerous, it continues to save a growing number of lives.

Above *Christiaan Barnard speaks about his work on heart surgery in front of a television audience in 1968.*

Below *Barnard and his team of surgeons carrying out a heart transplant operation.*

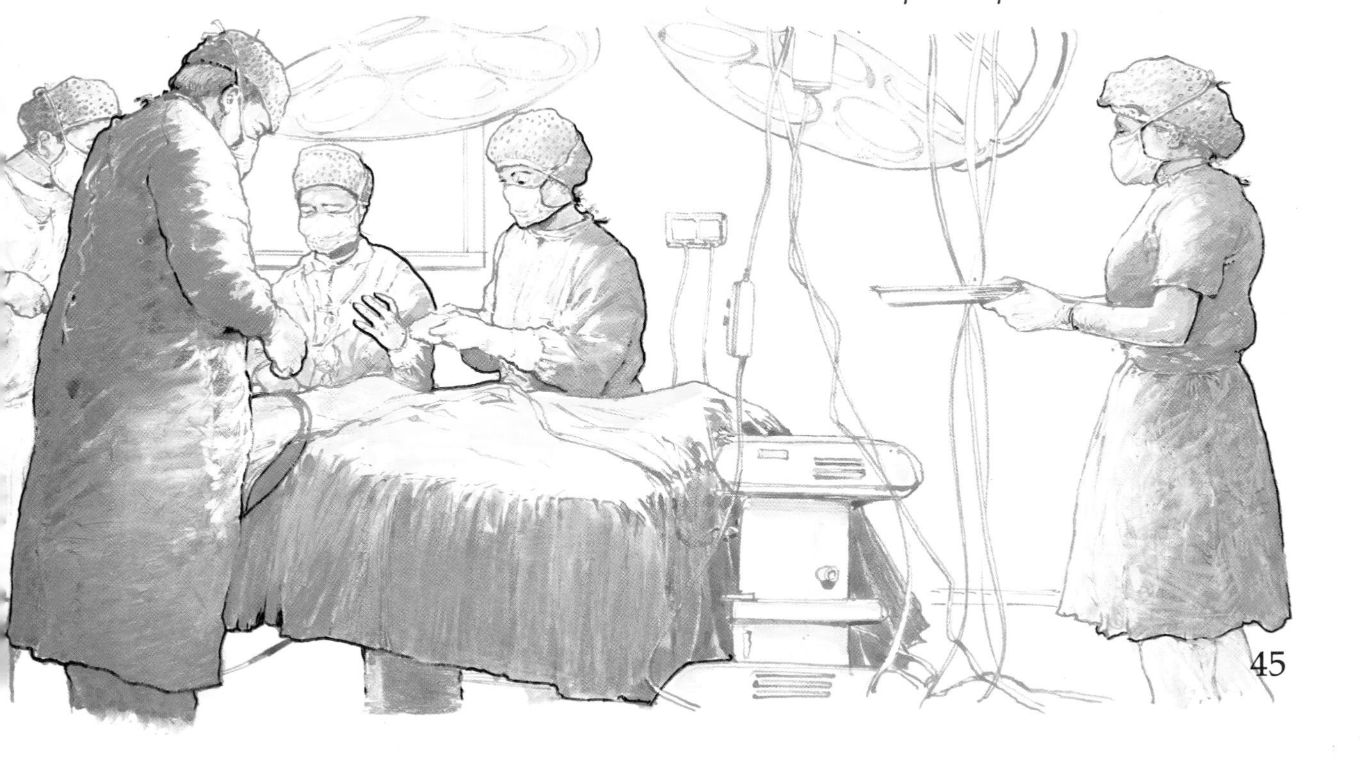

Glossary

Alchemist A person who, in ancient times, tried to turn base metals into gold.

Anatomy The science concerned with the structure of the body.

Anesthetic A substance given to a person to cause temporary loss of consciousness.

Antibiotics Chemical substances made by bacteria, used to stop the growth of other, harmful bacteria.

Antibodies Substances produced in the blood to fight harmful bacteria.

Apothecary The old word for a druggist.

Bacteria Microscopic organisms which can cause disease.

Cathode rays Electrically charged particles.

Culture Experimental growth of micro-organisms.

Dispensary A clinic where medicines can be obtained.

Dissection The process of taking a body apart in order to study it.

Epidemic Widespread outbreak of a disease.

Herbalist Someone skilled in the use of medicinal herbs.

Hypnosis A sleep-like state which has been artifically induced.

Inoculate To give a person a mild form of a disease by injecting bacteria to prevent a real attack.

Leprosy A chronic infectious disease occurring mainly in tropical areas of the world.

Midwifery The branch of nursing concerned with delivering babies and caring for women in childbirth.

Neurologist A doctor who specializes in diseases of the nervous system.

Nobel Prize The highest award for achievement in a particular field, awarded annually.

Organism All living animals or plants, including bacteria and viruses.

Vaccine A substance made from the virus that causes a disease.

Virus An orangism smaller than bacteria, which causes some diseases.

Further reading

The Art of Medicine by Tom Glass (Glass Publishing Co, 1986)

Bacteria: How They Affect Other Living Things by Dorothy H. Patent (Holiday House, 1980)

Breakthrough: The True Story of Penicillin by Francine Jacobs (Dodd, Mead, 1985)

Childbirth by Philip Rhodes (Carolina Biological Supply Co, 1980)

Disease and Discovery by Eva Bailey (David & Charles, 1985)

Florence Nightingale by Dorothy Turner (Watts, Franklin, 1986)

Goodbye to Bedlam: Understanding Mental Illness and Retardation by John Langone (Little, Brown & Co, 1974)

How Did We Find Out about Blood by Isaac Asimov (Walker & Co, 1986)

The Last Hundred Years: Medicine by Daniel Cohen (M. Evans & Co, 1981)

Louis Pasteur: Young Scientist by Francene Sabin (Troll Associates, 1983)

Medical Ethics by Carl Heintze (Watts, Franklin, 1987)

Microbes and Bacteria by Francene Sabin (Troll Associates, 1985)

Viruses: Life's Smallest Enemies by David C. Knight (William Morrow & Co, 1981)

Index

Picture acknowledgements

Camerapix 41; Mary Evans 23, 31, 33, 35; Mansell 21, 29; Peter Newark's Western Americana 25; Ann Ronan 9, 11, 15, 17, 27; The Research House 39; Topham Picture Library 37, 43, 45; Wayland Picture Library 13.

S0-EDL-052

Rise of the Raj

PEGGY WOODFORD

Rise of the Raj

MIDAS BOOKS, SPELDHURST, KENT / HUMANITIES PRESS INC., ATLANTIC HIGHLANDS, NEW JERSEY

First published in UK in 1978 by
Midas Books
12 Dene Way, Speldhurst,
Tunbridge Wells, Kent TN3 0NX

ISBN 0 85936 098 9 (UK Edition)

First published in USA in 1978 by
Humanities Press Inc.
Atlantic Highlands,
New Jersey 07716

LIBRARY OF CONGRESS CATALOGING IN PUBLICATION DATA
Woodford, Peggy.
Rise of the Raj.

Bibliography: p.
Includes index.
1. India – History – British occupation, 1765-1947.
2. India – History – 1500-1765. 3. British in India.
I. Title.
DS463.W66 954'.004'21 78-4211
ISBN 0-391-00867-6

Designed and produced by
Mechanick Exercises, London

Set in Monotype Baskerville by
South Bucks Typesetters Ltd.
Beaconsfield

Reproduction by Pembury Litho
Plates Ltd. Pembury,
Tunbridge Wells

Printed in Great Britain by
Chapel River Press, Andover

To the memory of my grandfather and my father, who served their lives as civilians in India, and to my brothers, who did not have that option

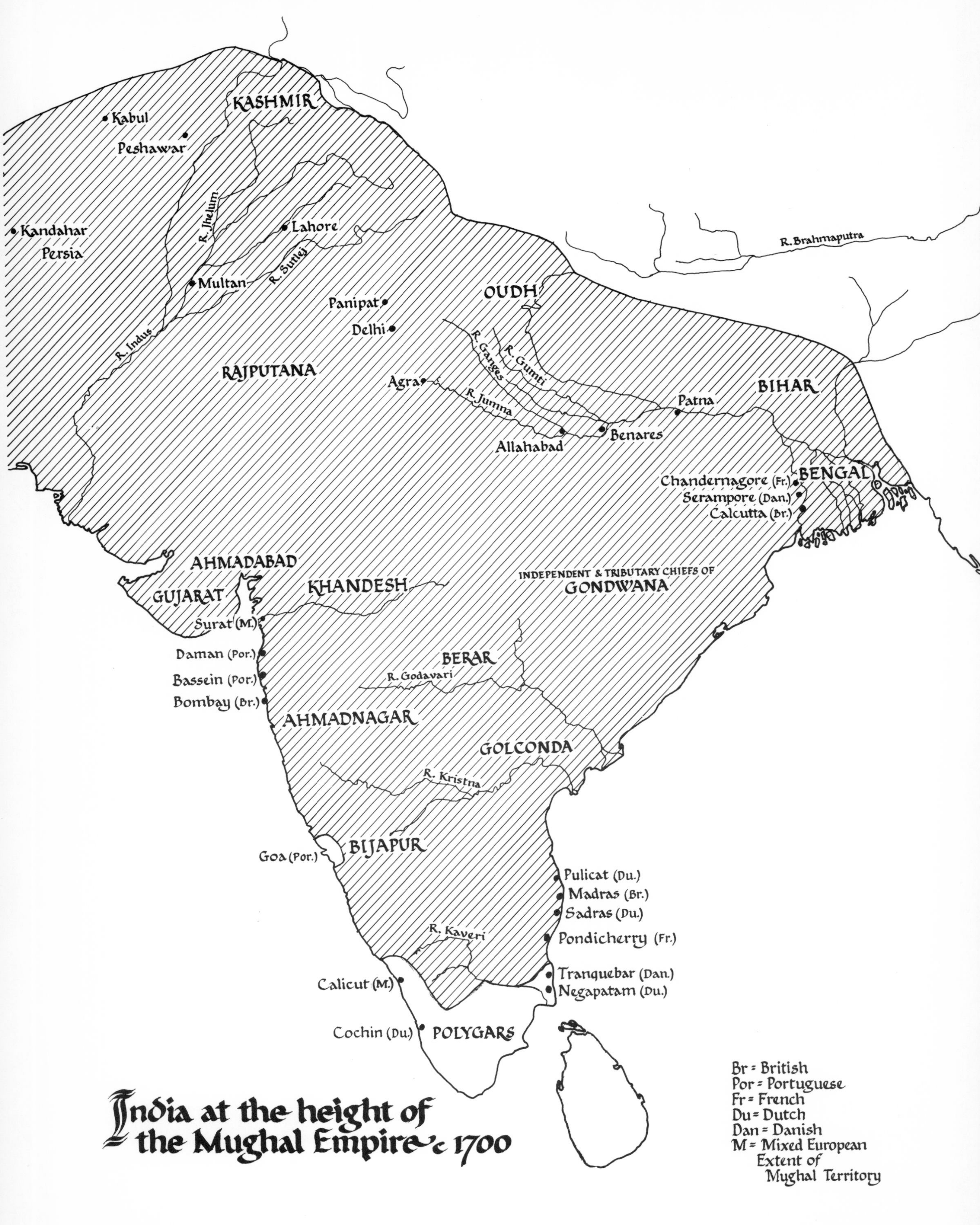

India at the height of the Mughal Empire c 1700

India on the eve of the Mutiny 1856

Contents

Illustrations

COLOUR PLATES (*between pages 80 and 81*)

My Tents, 1840. Watercolour by J. B. Bellasis from his *Scrapbook 1822-56.* (India Office Library)

Government House. Coloured aquatint by James Baillie Fraser (1810-60). (Victoria and Albert Museum)

The Jarakeshwar murder trial. Watercolour, Kalighat, *c.* 1875. (Victoria and Albert Museum)

The Raja of Tanjore. 24-foot scroll painting ,tempera on paper affixed to cloth, *c.* 1830. (Victoria and Albert Museum)

Indian Gerbils. Drawing by native artist, Barrackpore, *c.* 1805. (India Office Library)

Lucknow, 1860. Painting by William Simpson (1823-99). (Victoria and Albert Museum)

The Young Ladies' Toilet. Illustration from William Tayler's *Sketches Illustrating the Manners and Customs of the Indian and Anglo-Indians*, London, 1842. (Victoria and Albert Museum)

Ootacamund. Plate IV from Captain Richard Barron's *Views in India chiefly among the Neelgherry Hills taken during a short residence on them in 1835.* (Victoria and Albert Museum)

Captain John Johnson. Self-portrait in watercolour, 1801. (India Office Library)

Lieutenant-Colonel W. R. Gilbert and other British officers. Watercolour by a Calcutta artist in the employ of Lieutenant-Colonel Gilbert, *c.* 1825. (India Office Library.)

Foreword

It is said that if one has been born in India a little of its potent dust gets into one's bones, and that certainly seems true in the understanding and vision with which Peggy Woodford has written *Rise of the Raj*.

She quotes Philip Woodruff's remark that 'You must fly over India if you want to see how it is put together', and she has given us the same panoramic and comprehensive view of the rise, and the reign, of the British Raj; but she also has evoked what cannot be seen from the air, the countless intricate and fascinating details which make up the rich mosaic of this extraordinary story, and it *is* extraordinary – the rise from a small trading company to a vast empire. I am astonished at the sheer compass of Miss Woodford's research and equally impressed by the clarity with which she has told her tale.

Above all she has been fair – refreshing when, among so many modern young writers, it has been fashionable to sneer at the British Raj – and smear it – but then Peggy Woodford, though both young and modern, is something they are not; she could be called 'pedigree' Raj, because not only her father and mother, but her grandfather and grandmother were typical examples of the best of its selfless and wise service. They would have been proud of her talent and even prouder of the balanced and illuminating way in which she has written this book.

Rumer Godden.

Acknowledgments

I should like to express my thanks to Dr Judith Brown, Lecturer in History at Manchester University and to Dr Richard Bingle of the India Office Library and Records for their help and advice; to Mildred Archer and Pauline Rohatgi of the Prints and Drawings Room at the India Office Library for their assistance in my picture research; to Peter Southwell-Sander for his constructive criticism of the text; to Betty Tyers of the Indian Section at the Victoria and Albert Museum whose painstaking help has been invaluable; and finally to Hartnoll and Eyre Limited, of St James's, whose specialist knowledge is always so generously given.

1 Fortune in the East

In 1592, the English captured a large Portuguese ship, the *Madre de Dios*, full of Indian cargo; when the cargo was listed and valued in London its size, richness and variety amazed the English merchants. The ship contained £150,000 worth of valuables, including jewels, spices, silks, calicoes, carpets, quilts, dyes, porcelain vessels and rarities like elephants' teeth and coconuts. Now merchants became increasingly determined to open up commerce in the East, formed the East India Company and pressed for a Royal Charter to trade where the rewards seemed so large.

Almost exactly three hundred years later, an Englishman called John Beames who owed his presence and his job in India to that same East India Company (by then defunct) was to write enthusiastically: 'Governing men is grand work, the noblest of all occupations though perhaps the most difficult.' Commerce and profit were dirty words to men like him; he was in India to maintain the Raj, Her Majesty's Empire in the East. That this Empire grew out of trade was something the later Victorians preferred to forget.

How a trading company came to found a successful empire is one of the most exciting stories in British history. Many complex factors caused the growth of this dominion, but one of the most important was the Mughal Empire itself.

When the British first arrived in India to trade, they found the Mughals, Muslims from Persia, ruling an Empire that was powerful, rich and well organized. Hindu India had for a hundred years been subject to them, and the British regarded the mighty Mughal Empire with respect. They needed the Mughals' permission to trade, but beyond that they wanted no political involvement with either Muslim or Hindu. However, despite its solidly powerful appearance, the Mughal Empire had reached its peak and was beginning to decline, and this decline caused a vacuum which the British were eventually to fill.

The Mughals were a vivid and fascinating people. The word 'Mughal' itself requires explanation: it was the Persian word for 'Mongol' and was misused by the Indians to describe *all* invading foreigners from the North – Persians, Afghans or Mongols. Babur, the first of the great Mughal Emperors in India, would have hated to be known as a 'Mughal' since it was the Mongols who had driven him out of his Persian kingdom and caused him to try his luck in India.

Babur came to India in the early sixteenth century and defeated the Turks

List, dated 22 September 1599, of subscriptions promised for the first voyage of the East India Company by the Cape Route. The merchants listed raised £30,133 3s. 8d. and immediately applied for a charter. The request was not granted because negotiations were in progress to end the war with Spain and the government did not want to jeopardise them. After they had fallen through, the East India scheme was again put to the government, the merchants having more than doubled their first subscription in the meantime.

6

The names of suche persones as have written with there owne handes, to venter in the pretended voiage to the Easte Indies (the whiche it maie please the Lorde to prosper) and the Somes that they will adventure the xxij. Septembr. 1599. viz

1 Sr. Stephen Soame. Lo. Mayor London £ . 200 . 0 . 0
2 Sr. John Harte and George Bowles — £ 1000 . 0 . 0
3 Sr. John Spencer knight — £ . 800 . 0 . 0
4 Mr. Nicholas Mosley alderman — £ . 300 . 0 . 0
5 Mr. Paule Bayninge alderman — £ 1000 . 0 . 0
6 Mr. Leonarde Hallyday alderman — £ 1000 . 0 . 0
7 Mr. Richard Goddard alderman — £ . 200 . 0 . 0
8 Mr. John Moore alderman — £ . 300 . 0 . 0
9 Sr. Stephen Soame. Richd Cater — £ . 400 . 0 . 0
10 Mr. Edward Holmeden alderman — £ . 500 . 0 . 0
11 Mr. Roberte Hampson alderman — £ . 300 . 0 . 0
12 Mr. Richard Staper — £ . 500 . 0 . 0
13 Mr. Thomas Symonds — £ . 200 . 0 . 0
14 Mr. John Eldred. — £ . 400 . 0 . 0
15 Robarte Coxe grocer — £ . 250 . 0 . 0
16 Nicholas Leatt yremonger — £ . 200 . 0 . 0
17 Thomas Garwaye draper — £ . 200 . 0 . 0
18 George Holman grocer. — £ . 150 . 0 . 0
19 Thomas Hicrocks. — £ . 100 . 0 . 0
20 Robarte Sandye grocer — £ . 200 . 0 . 0
21 Nicholas Pearde clotheworker — £ . 100 . 0 . 0
22 Thomas Edwardes. — £ . 200 . 0 . 0
23 Nicholas Barnesley grocer — £ . 150 . 0 . 0
24 William Dale. — £ . 100 . 0 . 0
25 Nicholas Lingo — £ . 100 . 0 . 0
26 Nicholas Style grocer — £ . 200 . 0 . 0
27 Lawrence Greene — £ . 200 . 0 . 0
28 Edwarde Collins clotheworker — £ . 200 . 0 . 0
29 Frauncis Cherie vinteneer — £ . 200 . 0 . 0
30 Oliver Style grocer — £ . 300 . 0 . 0
31 Richarde and Jeames Wyche — £ . 200 . 0 . 0
32 Thoms and Robte Midleton Robt Bateman £ . 500 . 0 . 0
33 Nicholas Farrer skynner — £ . 200 . 0 . 0
34 Fraunces Terrell. — £ . 200 . 0 . 0
35 Thoms Farrington, vintener — £ . 200 . 0 . 0
36 Richard Wragge — £ . 200 . 0 . 0

Borne over £ 11450 . 0 . 0

The Emperor Babur (1483-1530, ruled 1526-30). This portrait, done during Shah Jehan's reign (1627-58), is thought to be a copy of an earlier portrait.

and Afghans who already held power there. (India is used to empires being imposed on her by foreign invaders; it has happened constantly throughout her history.) By 1526 Babur had control of most of Hindustan, but he died in 1530 before he could stabilize peace. Babur's conquest of north India was a triumph of personality; his resources were small, his enemies formidable and his fellow-Persians far from enthusiastic about India. Yet he held them all loyal by his wit, good temper and robust sense of humour. His standard of honour, for his period, was high; he was a sophisticated, perceptive man with a deep appreciation of all the arts and a love of nature. His first act on reaching Agra, the capital, was to lay out a garden (still in existence as the Ram Bagh). He was a fine poet, and his prose memoir is a masterpiece of clarity and perspective. Here is his reaction to his new empire:

> Hindustan is a country that has few pleasures to recommend it. The people are not handsome. They have no idea of the charms of friendly society, of frankly mixing together, or a familiar intercourse. They have no genius, no comprehension of mind, no politeness of manner, no kindness or fellow-feeling, no ingenuity or mechanical invention in planning or executing their handicraft works, no skill or knowledge in design or architecture; they have no horses, no good flesh, no grapes or musk-melons, no good fruits, no ice or cold water, no good food or bread in their bazaars, no baths or colleges, no candles, no torches, not a candlestick.

From this list of things lacking, we can see what richness the Mughals brought with them. Babur was a Muslim, but not a fanatical one; he did not interfere with the religion of the Hindus. His arrival did India nothing but good:

> Babur's is a humane and gracious as well as an adventurous figure; he sheds a ray of light upon scenes of violence and perfidy, which make up so much of early sixteenth-century politics in this part of the world.

So Spear in his history of India describes Babur. He also gives a very vivid description of Akbar the Great, Babur's grandson, who reigned from 1556 to 1605:

> Akbar is one of the most famous characters in Indian history and also one of the most complex. It is traditional even today, in the north Indian countryside, to attribute to him anything great or good, as anything unpopular tends to be attributed to Aurangzeb. He excelled in many fields. As a soldier he was noted for his lightning marches. In 1573 he covered six hundred miles in twenty-one days to surprise rebels who could not believe it was the emperor who was among them. He was an administrator of genius with the faculty of co-ordinating and inspiring the work of others. He was a leader of renown, who could inspire as well as command, and secure willing obedience from devotion as well as by fear. He was a statesman with large views who understood the art of conciliation. He was an intellectual who delighted in knowledge of all kinds, in theological argument and philosophical discussion. His inability to read, so often quoted, was no sign of the barbarism of the age, but a case of successful wilfulness during a hazardous and vagrant youth. Authority came to him at the age of thirteen, when he was able to substitute readers and writers for the personal practice of these arts. He had a refined artistic taste which stamped itself on the arts of painting and architecture. He had, with occasional fits of Mongol rage, a generous disposition and a humane temper. Executions in his reign were few and he attempted to alleviate the miseries of famine. Above all, he possessed a personal

Late sixteenth-century painting of the Emperor Babur enthroned in one of the gardens he made in India.

Portrait, probably of Akbar the Great (1542-1605). This unusual drawing shows the high standards reached by the Mughal court artists.

magnetism which drew men unto him. . . . His name became a legend in his lifetime, not because of the length of his reign or the extent of his conquests nor even because he mixed humanity with his statecraft or generosity with his triumphs, but because of that something extra in the make-up, that flash of the eye or turn of the head, which marks the crossing of the gulf between ability and genius. Queen Elizabeth had it and so had Abraham Lincoln. It has been the hallmark of supreme gifts in all ages.

It was Akbar's work of integration and organization which so particularly prepared for British rule in India. In Akbar's time, Muslims were a tiny minority compared with the existing population of Hindus. Akbar enlisted Hindu support for his rule by giving their leaders equal status with the Muslims. To show he meant it, he married an Indian Raja's daughter, who became the mother of the next emperor, Jahangir. The emperor became protector of all

Nineteenth-century engraving of the Taj Mahal, built by the Emperor Shah Jehan.

his people and guardian of both religions. India was stable and, despite the gulf between the nature of the two religions, presented one face to the world.

But it was Akbar's administrative organization which most affected Indian life and gave the future pattern to British local government in India. He divided up the large states into a network of districts, each with its own decentralized administration of a governor (*subadar*) and a collector of revenue (*diwan*); these *subadars* and *diwans* were moved every four years or so, to prevent corruption. It was a highly efficient system, later used by the British very successfully.

A final achievement, again of value to the British, was the re-grading and re-classifying of land revenue. The new records were kept in every village and collections were made by imperial officers. Order was brought out of chaos. Without Akbar's efficient reforms, British administrators in the early nineteenth century would have had an impossible task; the Mughal system gave the British a real basis to build on.

Akbar's reign was also important culturally. He was an enthusiast for things Persian. Persian became the polite language of the whole of India. Persian manners and elegance of dress spread from Delhi all over India; Hindus learnt Persian methods of painting and there grew up as a result the famous school of Mughal miniaturists. Persian architecture blended in with Hindu traditions to form the Mughal style, of which the Taj Mahal is the supreme example. Persian gardens can be seen throughout India.

The seventeenth century was the golden age of the Mughal Empire. Its fame spread all over the western world; travellers came back with tales of real splendour and wealth, confirmed as we have seen by ships' cargoes like that of the *Madre de Dios*. The personalities of the emperors themselves helped to spread the legends; Akbar was followed by another striking and vivid man, his son Jahangir.

Jahangir was quite different from Akbar. He was a man of extremes: genial good humour and demonic temper; acute artistic sensibility and callous disregard for human suffering. He could not read or write but was well educated; his memoirs (presumably dictated) are as vivid and impressive in their own way as Babur's. Painting flourished at his court; so did corruption, as all the travellers testify. Jahangir remained, behind his outward conformity to Islam, a free thinker; he refused to identify the state with any particular religion. He continued to expand the Mughal Empire, though not so energetically as his great father; he ruled for twenty-two years, dying in 1627. He was succeeded by Shah Jehan and then by Aurangzeb; between them these two emperors ruled until 1707. Although there were eleven Mughal emperors in the remaining century and a half of the Empire, Aurangzeb was the last who could be called great.

Jahangir is particularly important because he had to deal with a flood of new travellers from Europe, all demanding trading rights. He had to choose between the rival merits of Portuguese, English and Dutch; the one he chose would be vitally important for that country's future development in India. The Portuguese put a great deal of pressure on him: they had arrived in India at the same time as Babur, in search of 'Christians and spices'. They were strong at sea, and they controlled the Muslim pilgrim route to Mecca. This was a very lucrative business, and it irked the Mughals to be so much at their mercy; thus rival sea powers were of great interest to Jahangir. When the first official representative of the East India Company, Captain William Hawkins, came to see him about trading rights, he was a welcome visitor not because of the trade he might bring but because English ships looked strong and efficient.

Little did Jahangir know that this East India Company was to found an empire greater than his own. The growth of a political and territorial empire from a purely commercial venture, a trading company, is unparalleled in world history. The Portuguese, Dutch and French were all very active in the East during this period, but it was the English who founded an empire.

In a strange way, it was the Dutch who brought about the British Raj (*Raj* is the Hindi word for 'kingdom' or 'rule'). The English wanted to capture a part of the spice trade, but the Dutch East India Company had already established strong settlements in the East Indies and were determined not to give up their monopoly of the spice trade. (There was a perpetual heavy demand for spices for the preservation and flavouring of food.) India was definitely second-best in the spice trade, but because the powerful Dutch company, with eight times the capital of the English company, denied the English access to the main spice centre in the East Indies (modern Indonesia), the English had no choice but to turn their attention to India.

On the last day of the year 1600, Queen Elizabeth I had given the East India Company their charter to trade containing the resounding words: 'as well for the honour of this our realm of England as for the increase of our navigation and advancement of trade . . .'. In March 1607, the Company sent 'our loving friend William Hawkins' in a 500-ton ship called the *Hector* to India; Hawkins carried a letter from King James I to the Mughal leader asking for permission to trade. Sixteen months later the *Hector* anchored off the Bombay coast.

It was clear from the start that local Mughal officials had no interest whatever in promoting trade; Hawkins could get no answer when he sought permission to build a 'factory' (a warehouse for storing goods). Eventually he was told that only the Emperor Jahangir himself could give permission; and the Mughal court was at Agra, a two months' journey away. Undaunted, Hawkins engaged fifty native horsemen for protection and set out with his party on 1 February 1609.

In his book *The Men Who Ruled India* Philip Woodruff has described beautifully what Hawkins would have seen of this new country:

> The road he saw on his journey when the first light came to show him the way – for he started early – is a road still to be found in every district of India. It is a road of earth, very broad, so that there is plenty of room to go round a bad patch in the rains. It is striped in the early morning light by long shadows where the wheels have worn deep ruts in the pearly dust; it is flanked on either side by an intermittent hedge of cactus and tall plumes of elephant grass. In these first minutes of the day the dust is still too moist with dew to rise high above the ground; all is still clear and sweet. There are lines of camels pulling tall carts like gipsy caravans, droves of patient little grey-white cattle and black sullen buffaloes going to graze, a peasant carrying his shoes on the end of his bamboo pole to save leather, a potter with his donkeys, traffic that will not change much in three hundred years.
>
> Nor will the fields on either side of the road be very different then and now. In Hawkins's day as now there will be black partridges calling in the wheat and barley; the crops will be fresh and green, as high as the calf of a man's leg, heavy with dew. There will be grey partridges running in the tall pulse called *arhar* and among the little chick-pea known as *gram*. There will be blackbuck wandering between the plots of cotton and pepper; men will be beginning to cut into the squares of sugar-cane that still bristle with pike-heads as defiant as clusters of Spanish infantry. Only there will be more opium and poppy in Hawkins's day and near Agra there will be indigo.

Since it is February they will be working the wells and, not long after the sun is up, Hawkins will hear an inconsequent little song, rising and falling in a recitative more like a lark's than a man's; it is the song of the man who catches the great leather bag the bullocks have dragged up from the depths of the well, catches and swings it glistening over the watercourse to spill its cool glittering burden on the fields.

Hawkins finally arrived at Agra in mid-April, alas minus all the presents destined to soften the Emperor – all had been stolen from him. He also found that his letter of introduction had to be translated into Persian by a Portuguese Jesuit attached to the court: not exactly a reliable translator. But Hawkins made up for these disadvantages by the fact that he spoke Turkish, learnt when he was a merchant in the Levant, and Turkish was the familiar, as opposed to the court, language of the emperors. So Hawkins could talk to the Emperor himself without need of an interpreter: an unusual state of affairs and perhaps one of the main reasons why Jahangir took such a fancy to this engaging

Sir Thomas Roe (1581?-1644), a portrait by an unknown seventeenth-century artist. After his Indian voyage he was sent as ambassador to a wide variety of places, including Constantinople, Sweden, Poland and Vienna. In knowledge of foreign affairs and of the details of British commerce he probably had no living equal.

Mercator's map of India, from an edition which Sir Thomas Roe presented to Jahangir. The Emperor, at first very pleased, later returned the map, perhaps, says Roe's chaplain Terry, because it was too much of a shock to discover how much of the world remained for him to conquer.

Late Victorian drawing-room tent. The elaborate mirror behind the sofa gives a final touch to the illusion of solidity. No wonder Vice-regal baggage trains were so long.

character. Hawkins was invited to stay at the Mughal court as long as he liked, was given an imperial post as a commander, was in intimate daily conversation with Jahangir, and finally had the honour of being offered a concubine:

> the king was very earnest with me to take a white maiden out of his palace; he would give her all things necessary with slaves and he would promise me she should turn Christian, and by this means my meats and drinks should be looked to and I should live without fear of the Jesuits' poison.

Hawkins insisted that his woman had to be a genuine Christian; Jahangir 'called to memory' a certain Armenian Christian, daughter of one of Akbar's captains, and Hawkins married her. He adopted an oriental life-style and dressed in Muslim clothes; perhaps it was just as well that the East India Company authorities were too far away to know what their envoy was up to. But Hawkins had not forgotten the reason for his presence at the Mughal court; he continued to press Jahangir for a decision. However the Portuguese Jesuits, besides plotting against the Englishman's life, managed to sabotage all his diplomatic arrangements with the Mughals. Jahangir blew hot and cold; the Portuguese desperately intrigued to keep the English out; Hawkins, enjoying his new life, bided his time. But eventually he fell from favour and, leaving the treacherous, corrupt court, returned with his wife to England. He died on the journey home; no one knows what became of the Armenian girl.

It is interesting that the first close contact between English and Indian was such an atypical one. Some later Englishmen were to adopt an oriental way of life, but none had such access to the Emperor as Hawkins did. Yet he achieved little for the advancement of trading rights; he had become too involved with his hosts and lacked the dignity and nobility of character needed to exact their respect.

These were qualities which the aristocratic Sir Thomas Roe, King James' ambassador to the court of Jahangir, had in good measure. He was far more typical of later British India than Hawkins; his whole attitude and bearing remind one of the great statesmen in India in the nineteenth century. Roe arrived in India in 1615, hoping to negotiate a treaty between the two sovereigns; he insisted from the start that he should be treated correctly, with due decorum as the King's representative, and he was. He combined the best and the less appealing characteristics of the English; he was 'of a pregnant understanding, well-spoken, learned, industrious and of a comely personage'; he was inflexible, solemn and a little pompous, and unsympathetic to other ways of living than his own. He wrote home of India: 'this is the dullest basest place that ever I saw and maketh me weary of speaking of it.'

This was a sentiment many English were to make after him. 'I cannot abide India,' said Emily Eden, sister of the Governor Lord Auckland, two hundred years later. Another Victorian remarked: 'You know I never liked India, but one always takes a sort of stoical pleasure in doing a very unpleasant duty.' Roe obviously agreed in part with the last remark; his distaste contrasts strongly with Hawkins' evident appreciation of the country. Hawkins is more representative of the majority of the British who went to India; most people became deeply attached to her despite the drawbacks.

Thomas Roe spent three years in India; during this time he, like Hawkins, kept a diary, which gives us a most vivid and unexaggerated picture of life at Jahangir's court. He is more detached from events than Hawkins and sees things more clearly. He understood, for instance, the power of Jahangir's wife, Nur Jehan, although of course he never saw her because no Muslim women

Camp scene. Illustration from the *Journal* of Captain Robert Smith, late H.M. 44th Regiment. Captain Smith joined the 44th Regiment as an Ensign in 1809. The Regiment went to India in 1822; Smith became a Captain three years later and left the Regiment in 1833. The delicate pencil drawings which illustrate his hand-written *Journal* are exceptionally fine.

Camp Scene in Oudh, c. 1820. The servants' tents are on the right, officers' on the left. The hat-box-like containers are carried in pairs on the ends of poles by bearers.

except dancing girls were ever seen by men other than their own husbands. Roe wrote to the Governor of the East India Company: 'all justice or care of any thing or public affairs either sleeps or depends on her, who is more inaccessible than any goddess or mystery of heathen impiety.' Roe also saw the political structure of the court very clearly; he analyzed the Mughal King as:

every man's heir, which maketh him rich and the country evil builded. The great men about him are not born noble but favourites raised; to whom . . . he assigneth so much land . . . but as they die . . . so it returneth to the King, like rivers to the sea.

Here is Roe's vivid description of the great Jahangir:

The King descended the stairs with such an acclamation of 'health to the King' as would have out-cried cannons. At the stair's foot, where I met him, and shuffled to be next, one brought a mighty carp; another a dish of white stuff like starch, into which he put his finger, and touched the fish and so rubbed it on his forehead, a ceremony used presaging good fortune. Then another came and buckled on his sword and buckler, set all over with great diamonds and rubies, the belts of gold suitable. . . . On his head he wore a rich turban with a plume of heron tops, not many but long; on one side hung a ruby unset, as big as a walnut; on the other side a diamond as great; in the middle an emerald like a heart, much bigger. His sash was wreathed about with a chain of great pearl, rubies, and diamonds drilled. About his neck he carried a chain of most excellent pearl, three double (so great I never saw); at his elbows, armlets set with diamonds; and on his wrists three rows of several sorts. His hands bare, but on almost every finger a ring; his gloves, which were English, stuck under his girdle.

How pleased Roe was as he 'shuffled to be next' to find his present of English gloves tucked into all that finery; he had already complained bitterly to the East India Company of their shoddy presents to the Emperor, which had not gone down at all well. Roe knew as well as everyone did who sought for imperial favour that presents were all-important. Luckily an English coach, sent out in pieces, pleased Jahangir, although he immediately had the upholstery

East encounters West under a vast Banyan Tree. Illustration from James Forbes' *Oriental Memoirs*, 1778.

replaced with a much richer brocade and the brass nails changed for silver ones!

Roe travelled with the Emperor and has left invaluable descriptions of a royal camp, 'one of the wonders of my little experience', as he puts it. It took twelve hours for the whole procession to pass any one place, and Roe calculated that when halted it covered an area twenty miles round. It was organized like a town, with regular streets where each noble or tradesman had his allotted place, so that wherever it was established the camp was identical and people could find their way around. The King and nobles had two sets of tents, one of

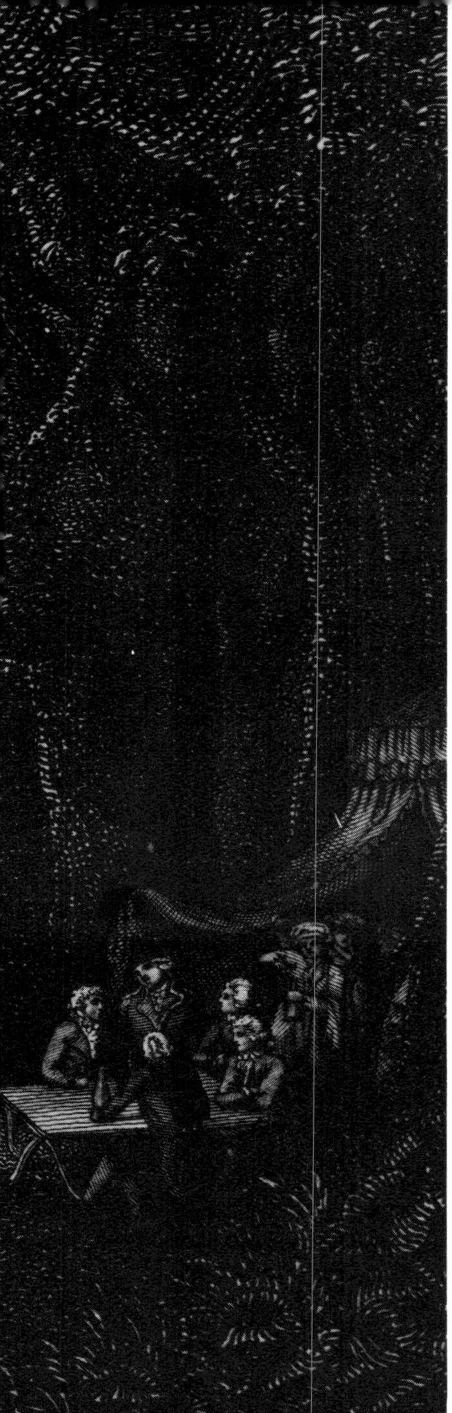

which was sent ahead to be ready for them on arrival. British viceroys in India were later to travel about in exactly the same manner. Lord Auckland's imperial cavalcade in 1837 was twelve thousand strong, followed in turn by 'ten miles of beasts of burden' who carried tables, chairs, cupboards, beds, all the gear of the dressing-room, trunks filled with books, linen, silver and tableware. From what Roe says, though, Jahangir's tents outdid the British viceroys'. The latter had a vast network of tents containing private bedroom, sitting-room and dressing-room; these were linked to public dining-rooms and durbar rooms by covered ways. Jahangir's quarters were a fort of painted wood and canvas three hundred yards in diameter; in addition to all the usual public rooms and the essential harem was a travelling mosque.

Camping, simple or elaborate, has always been an important part of life in India; the distances were so vast that well-organized systems of camping developed early. One of the strengths of later British rule was the regular camping tours all *mofussil* (rural) civil servants undertook from the end of the eighteenth century onwards. And the magic of the Indian early morning is something that no one who has camped in India can forget; the crystalline freshness of the sun before the heat begins, the heightened scents of earth and grass, the smell of wood smoke as food and tea are prepared, a magic Bishop Heber of Calcutta captures in his description of camping in the early nineteenth century.

> The morning was positively cold and the whole scene, with the exercise of the march, the picturesque groups of men and animals round me – the bracing air, the singing of the birds, the light mist hanging on the trees, and the glistening dew was such that I have seldom found anything better adapted to raise a man's animal spirits and put him in a good temper with himself and all the world.

European seamen preparing to unload a shipment of bales in about 1680.

Despite his patient diplomacy, Roe did not achieve a full treaty between the English and the Mughal kings, but he did gain permission for the East India Company to trade throughout India. His chaplain, Edward Terry, who travelled with him to Agra, summed up Roe's achievements with Jahangir:

> There can be no dealing with this king upon very sure terms, for he will say and unsay, promise and deny. Yet we Englishmen did not at all suffer by that inconstancy of his, but there found a free trade, a peaceable residence and a very good esteem with that king and people.

Perhaps it was Roe's undoubted calibre that helped to make Jahangir, in the struggle between Portuguese and English for his favour, tip the balance towards the English. One cannot help feeling that in Jahangir's eyes the perfect solution would have been to ignore both these irritating foreigners completely. But they were strong maritime nations: Jahangir's hand was forced to form an agreement with either one or the other. Spear says in his history of India:

> His decision to prefer the British to the Portuguese required insight in the circumstances of the times. It was based on the East India Company's success against the Portuguese in the estuary of the Swally (near Surat) in 1613. From that time the company became virtual naval auxiliaries to the Moguls in return for trading privileges within the empire. Captain Hawkins gave Jahangir much pleasure as a boon companion between 1607 and 1611, but it was Sir Thomas Roe, who drank little and spoke no Persian, who achieved a lasting settlement.

In the huge hill fortress of Mandu is a summerhouse built in Akbar's time. Here Jahangir, with Sir Thomas Roe and his chaplain in his entourage, had a delightful picnic with his ladies. The snake spiral at the end of the pool in this summerhouse is of a peculiar beauty and seems to symbolize the relationship during the seventeenth century between the Mughals and the British. The two snake forms circle each other, but their heads do not touch; the water of ordinary Indian life flows shaped by the conduit they form. As Spear says: 'there was a meeting of mutual curiosity, but not a marriage of true minds.'

Spiral water-duct in the Nilkanth summer-house at Mandu, built in Akbar the Great's time.

2 From Nabob to Sahib

For the first hundred years, the British settled only on the edges of India; one after another the necessary small trading settlements were formed, linked to each other mainly by coastal routes. The vast hinterland was known to very few; trade was confined to the coast. The powerful Mughals ruled inland, and most East India Company officials continued to have a healthy respect for Mughal domination and government.

The largeness of India makes one marvel at the maintenance of any cohesive empire there before the days of speedy communication. Seventeenth-century India contained a few main routes or tracks, but large areas remained wilderness or jungle. The rivers were mainly unbridged: they could be forded in dry weather and crossed by ferry during the monsoon. The horse, camel or bullock cart determined the pace of travel; it took for instance up to three months to get from the Mughal capital, Agra, to Bengal. Central India was too rough except for packhorses or men on foot. Yet the Emperor Aurangzeb continued to expand his empire southwards; distances and difficult terrain did not deter him. However, its unwieldy size made it difficult to administer and brought weakness and then decay.

An excellent description of the sub-continent's overall shape and variety is given by Philip Woodruff, always so sensitive to the real India:

> You must fly over India if you want to see how it is put together. From a train, there is not enough in the eye at one glance and it is gone too soon; by bullock-cart the journey takes too long; you have forgotten what you saw last week before you are in the next district.
>
> Fly from West to East, along the broad band of flat country that lies below the Himalayas. . . . You begin over windy plains of wheat, where the men might be Italians except that they are much bigger than Italians, where people eat wheat and milk and butter, and meat when they can get it. Fly on towards the East, a faint jagged arabesque of snowy dome and icy peak on your left, and now the rivers run the other way, towards the rising sun, and you are still over plains, very flat, sprinkled here and there with plump square pincushions of glossy green which are groves of mangoes. There are more little squares of brown now among the young wheat, where in a few months' time there will be the vivid, emerald green of rice. Fly on all day till you come down in the evening in a country where wheat is unknown, where rice and fish are what the people eat, where there are boats instead of bullock-carts.
>
> You have flown all day, from the Salt Range to the mouths of the Ganges and all

A Party of Europeans Carousing on a Terrace. This is probably an eighteenth-century copy by a Mughal artist of a sixteenth-century original, which in turn seems to have been based on a European original.

day the land has been a flat chess-board with tracks and waterways wriggling among the squares of cultivation; the only change has been in the people and in what they grow. At each halt, you met men a little darker and squatter than at the last, but beneath a different colouring, the shape of their features did not seem so very foreign, and the languages they spoke were all dialects of one tongue that was a cousin to Latin.

But if you had turned to the South, the Deccan, the country of the right hand, there would have been a change at once and you would have flown over a tangle of hills and forests, rocky rivers and gorges, ruined forts on red sandstone crags, temples with bloated spires and little lakes, a country of red rocks, red gravel and dark green foliage, sharp and garish after the almond-green and almond-buff plains of the

Surat in 1772. Under the Mughals, Surat was one of the main ports for trade and for the pilgrim traffic to Mecca. In 1613 Jahangir allowed the establishment of the first English 'factory' there. This was the headquarters of the East India Company until 1687, when the Presidency of the English factory was transferred to Bombay.

North. And you would have come down among a strange people, among Brahmins with the arched nostril, the sharp-bridged nose, of the temple carvings, among labourers with the heavier features and darker skin of the aboriginal, among people whose many tongues were . . . incomprehensible.

The English trader in the seventeenth century knew none of this; he simply battled against the physical difficulties presented by his little corner. He believed that Mughal power was absolute and was thankful for its stable rule. He also knew that the Mughals only preferred the British because their sea power was greatest. It was very simple – trading rights in return for protection. Or rather, it seemed simple; but even here lay the seeds of eventual British domination. Once a ruler relies on protection from another race, he lays himself open to possible subjection by that race. Much later on, Indian rulers hired soldiers from the East India Company at vast expense, thereby putting themselves forever in the debt of the British because they were never able to pay off the sums they owed.

If anyone had told those early Englishmen that their little patches of settlement were the first steps towards an empire far greater than the Mughals', it would have been beyond belief. They were only there for trade, and for the

View of Bombay in 1773.

efficient handling of it to everyone's maximum profit. Territory was a responsibility they had no wish to acquire. But unfortunately territory comes with trade: the settlement needs adequate space, the traders places to live, the suppliers in the villages around need protection, and so the process of encroachment begins.

The East India Company's first permanent factory was established at Surat near Bombay in 1613; by 1619, after Sir Thomas Roe's good offices at Jahangir's

court, there were factories at Broach, Agra and Ahmadabad as well. Roe left India in 1619 warning the East India Company not to waste their money on large garrisons and military expansion: 'if you will profit, seek it at sea, and in quiet trade: for without controversy it is an error to affect Garrisons and Land Wars in India.'

Though the Directors of the Company were in no doubt that 'quiet trade' with India would be lucrative and desirable, many English contemporaries had their doubts. In 1621 a pamphlet was published in London condemning the whole business:

1. It was a happie thing for Christendome (say many men) that the navigation to the East Indies, by way of the Cape of Good Hope, had never been found out; for in the fleets of shippes, which are sent thither yearly out of England, Portingall, and the low countries, the gold, silver, and coyne of Christendome, and particularly of this Kindome, is exhausted, to buy unnecessarie wares.

2. The timber, plancke, and other materials for making of shipping, is exceedinglie wasted, and made dearer, by the building of so many great shippes, as are yearly sent to trade in the East Indies; and yet the state hath no use of any of them upon occasion. For either they are not here; or else they come home verie weake and unserviceable.

3. The voyages to the East Indies do greatly consume our victuals, and our marriners leaving many poore widdowes and children unrelieved. Besides, that many shippes are yearely sent forth to the East Indies, and few we see as yet returned. Also this trade hath greatly decaied the traffique and shipping, which were wont to bee employed in the streights. And yet the said Trade of the East Indies, is found very unprofitable to the Adventurers. Neither doth the commonwealth finde any benefit by the cheapenesse of spice and Indigo, more than in times past.

4. It is generally observed, that His Majestie's Mint hath had but little employment ever sithence the East India Trade began; wherefore it is manifest, that the only remedie for this, and so many evils, besides, is to put downe this Trade. For what other remedy can there bee for the good of the commonwealth?

View of Bombay Green in 1763.

Watercolour from J. B. Bellasis' *Scrapbook 1822-56* of Bombay harbour from Malabar Hill. Many English people wanted to keep their own record of a residence in India and because of this urge there is a rich collection of amateur drawings and sketchbooks in the India Office Library; the value of these illustrated family diaries is immense, both historically and artistically. The drawings of J. B. Bellasis (1806-90) have a particular charm; his sense of colour was excellent. Bellasis served with the Bombay Army in west India and the Deccan from 1822 to 1856.

Luckily no one took any notice of the critics; though the English had put down the roots of trade in India, for over 150 years no one saw how huge a tree was to grow from them.

Several travellers who visited these early British settlements have left vivid descriptions of life in them. The merchants lived a collegiate life, with strict rules laid down by the Directors back in London – they clearly thought that these tiny isolated outposts needed a rigid structure for the good of trade as well as morale. The President at each settlement was king; a traveller to Surat in 1638 commented:

> The respect and deference which the other merchants have for the President was very remarkable, as also the order which was there observed in all things, especially at Divine Service, which was said twice a day, in the morning at six, and at eight at night, and on Sundays thrice. No person in the house but had his particular function, and their certain hours assigned them as well for work as recreation. . . . On Fridays after prayers, there was a particular assembly at which met with us three other merchants, who were of kin to the President . . . to make a commemoration and drink their wives' healths.

Their wives were not there with them: it was some years before Englishwomen were allowed to go out to India.

Another traveller, Peter Mundy, has left us pictures of what other settlements were like. He describes the English house at Agra:

Fort St George, Madras, painting after Jan van Ryne, *c.* 1754.

The honourable company have a house wherein their servants reside . . . in the heart of the city, where we live after this country in manner of meat, drink and apparel; . . . for the most part after the Custom of this place, sitting on the ground at our meat or discourse. The rooms in general covered with carpets with great round high cushions to lean on (this as well in public as in private). Our habit when we go abroad is a Shash (turban) on our heads, a white linen scarf over our shoulders, a fine white linen coat, a girdle to gird about us, breeches and shoes, our swords and daggers by our sides. Thus in the city. But when we go out of town, we have our bows and arrows at our saddle and a buckler hanging on our shoulders. However, we never stir a foot out of doors but on horseback, it being the custom of the city.

It is fascinating to see how those early Englishmen adopted oriental habits. But their efforts to adapt themselves did not lessen the mortality rate: Mundy found that of twenty-seven Englishmen at Surat only seven were alive six months later when he returned there, of whom three more were to die soon. Despite this depressing aspect of life in India, British traders continued to flock there in search of fortune and adventure. By 1647, there were twenty-three factories and ninety employees in all. Surat was the headquarters until Bombay came into British possession as part of the dowry of Catherine of Braganza when she married Charles II; in 1687 Bombay became the headquarters of the company on the West coast. Bombay had a good harbour but a bad climate. An early eighteenth-century writer, Captain Hamilton, was scathing about it:

Madras Landing, aquatint dating from 1837.

Madras Embarking, aquatint dating from 1837.

2 J

The ground is sterile and not to be improved. It has but little good Water on it and the Air is somewhat unhealthful, which is chiefly imputed to their dunging their Cocoanut Trees with Buckshoe, a Sort of small Fishes which their Sea abounds in. These being laid to the Roots of the Trees, putrefy, and cause a most unsavoury Smell; in the Mornings there is generally seen a thick Fog among those Trees that affects both the Brains and Lungs of Europeans and breeds Consumptions, Fevers and Fluxes.

The English died like flies; as a contemporary said: 'of every five hundred Europeans who came to live upon the Island not one hundred ever left it.'

Madras, founded on the East coast by the Company in 1639, on the first piece of territory officially granted to the British, had a better climate and prospered from the start. Madras seen from the sea as a traveller arrived fresh out from England was always thrilling: the ship would creep up the Coromandel coast with its palm trees and huge breakers until the gleaming houses and offices of Fort St George, Madras, came into view. Then small boats and catamarans would come out through the triple row of breakers and take all passengers and cargo ashore by stages. Most people were enthusiastic about Madras; an Englishmen, Ovington, wrote in 1710:

The prospect it gives is most delightful; nor appears it less magnificent by Land; the great Variety of fine Buildings that gracefully overlook its Walls, affording an inexpressible Satisfaction to a curious Eye. Towards the Land it is washed by a fruitful River that every November, half a Mile distant, discharges itself into the Sea, the Bar being first cut for its passage, which proceeding from the wet Monsoon, would otherwise occasion great Damage, by overflowing the adjacent Country. . . . The Streets are straight and wide, pav'd with Brick on each Side, but the Middle is deep Sand for carts to pass in: Where are no Houses are Causeways with trees on each side to supply the Defect. These being always green render it pleasant to those who otherwise must walk in the Sun. There are five Gates – the Sea, St. Thomas, Water, Choultry and Middle Gate. The Second and the Fourth may be opened for Passengers at any time of Night, if unsuspected, but neither of the other three after Six. The Publick Buildings are the Town Hall, St. Mary's Church, The College, New House and Hospital, with the Governor's Lodgings in the inner Fort. . . . The inhabitants enjoy perfect Health as they would do in England, which is plainly discovered by their ruddy Complexions; a good few of our other Settlements can boast. The Heats in Summer are the greatest Inconveniency they suffer under; yet I never heard of any ill effect from them. The delicious Fruits which the Country abounds with are a great Help in their Extremity; nor are they wanting to themselves in other Respects; Bathings and Wet Cloths being often apply'd with Success to the Relief of the Panting. It seldom lasts above four or five Hours in a day; when the Sea-breeze comes on, the Town seems to be new born. The Governor, during the Hot Winds, retires to the Company's new Garden for Refreshment, which he has made a very delightful Place of a barren one.

The first British venture to Bengal was made in 1633 by eight Englishmen who set sail up the East coast in a primitive junk 'with a high poop in it like a thatched house built in it for a cabin'. A Portuguese frigate did its unsuccessful best to prevent them; then the Chief Merchant, Ralph Cartwright, so impressed the Governor of Orissa by 'his confidence and fearless speech' that he secured full licence to trade. Slowly, settlements appeared in different parts of

View of Calicut on the coast of Malabar in 1772.

Bengal; the one at Hooghly was the most successful until nearby Calcutta itself was founded by Job Charnock.

Charnock was a man people did not forget, the epitome of the 'rough diamond'. During Charnock's time in Bengal the Mughal Emperor Aurangzeb was making trade almost impossible by exorbitant demands of taxes and 'presents'; at last the Mughals and the British came to the point of war. Charnock was a stubborn, determined man and with a very small force employed clever tactics against the Mughal thousands. For instance, a contemporary Indian describes this ruse:

> As he [Charnock] had a very small force and only one vessel was present at the time, while the Moghuls were assembled in great number, he saw no advantage in taking any hostile measure against them and was obliged to weigh anchor. He had a burning-glass in his ship, with which, by concentrating the sun's rays, he burnt the river face of the city.

Three quarters of Charnock's force had been killed or put out of action by the

Fort William, Calcutta, a painting after Jan van Ryne, *c.* 1754.

time the solitary vessel of the English reinforcement appeared. 'By an audacious use of trumpets, drums and loud huzzahs, Charnock deceived the enemy into believing that large reinforcements had arrived.' The Mughals sent a flag of truce. In the end Charnock and his men had to wait in Madras until the war with Aurangzeb was concluded, after which he returned to Bengal in triumph to found Calcutta, a city that flourished from the start. Charnock was a rough, tough trader, without birth or education to help him up the Company's ladder; but with his stubborn energy he achieved fame in his own way.

He also had a romantic side to him: he rescued a beautiful Brahmin widow from the flames of her husband's pyre, lived with her happily for fourteen years until her death, when he set up a magnificent tomb at which he sacrificed a cock every year. (This touch was Charnock's own brand of paganism.) He died in 1693, having 'reigned more absolutely than a Rajah, only he wanted much of their humanity'.

'Calcutta is the child of trade,' said the Reverend James Long, a Victorian resident there giving a history of the city. 'Charnock founded it with merchantile views on the eastern bank of the Hooghly, though the western was the more healthy; but there was a great number of weavers living at Suttanettee [the original site of Calcutta] and there was deep water.' Trade was the first consideration for all these early empire-builders. Captain Hamilton's witty description of Calcutta in the early eighteenth century also stresses its unhealthiness:

Calcutta and the Hooghly river in the mid-nineteenth century.

The English settled there about the year 1690, and after the Moghul had pardoned all the Robberies and Murders committed on his Subjects, Mr. Job Charnock, being then the Company's agent in Bengal, he had liberty to settle an Emporium in any part of the River's side below Hughly, and for the sake of a large shady tree chose that place, tho' he could not have chosen a more unhealthful place on all the River; for three miles to the North Eastern is a saltwater lake that overflows in September and October and then prodigious numbers of fish resort thither, but in November and December, when the floods are dissipated these fishes are left dry and with their putrefaction affect the air with thick stinking vapours, which the North-East Winds bring with them to Fort William, that they cause a yearly Mortality. Fort William was built an irregular Tetraon [*sic*] of brick and mortar called *Puckah*, which is a composition of Brick-dust, Lime Molasses and cut Hemp and is as hard as and tougher than firm Stone or Brick, and the Town was built without Order as the Builders thought most convenient for their own Affairs, everyone taking in what Ground most pleased them for Gardening so that in most houses you must pass through a Garden into the House, the English building near the River's Side and the Natives within Land. . . . About fifty yards from Fort William stands the Church built by the pious Charity of Merchants residing there. . . .

The Governor's house in the Fort is the most regular Piece of architecture that I ever saw in India. And there are many convenient Lodgings for Factors and Writers within the Fort and some storehouses for the Company's Goods and the Magazines for their Ammunition. The Company has a pretty good Hospital at Calcutta, where many go in to undergo the Penance of Physick but few come out to give account of its Operation. The Company has also a pretty good garden that furnishes the Governor's Table with Herbage and Fruits; and some Fish-ponds to serve his kitchen with good Carp, Calkrop and Mullet.

Shipping on the Hooghly river, Calcutta.

The Reverend Long goes into more detail about Calcutta's 'stinking vapours':

> We know not when Calcutta first got the title 'City of Palaces', though last century it was a misnomer in a place having no glass to its houses and few verandahs to shade off the heat; in whose streets dead animals were to be seen putrifying, and sometimes even human beings. Defective as are still the municipal arrangements of Calcutta, it is a great improvement on last century, when drains three feet deep were reservoirs of filth, sending out annually their three hundred and sixty stenches; the receptacle of rotting animals; even human corpses have been known to be two days in the streets, before being taken away by the police, and thrown into the canals.

No wonder that the death rate in Calcutta was as high as anywhere else. No one knew until the nineteenth century that water had anything to do with cholera, or mosquitoes with malaria. Much of the drinking water of Calcutta

A Weaver Working at the Loom: illustration from *The Cotton Fabrics of Bengal*, 1898.

for the first century and more of its existence was drawn from a large open pond in the middle of the city, where, to quote an eighteenth-century observer: 'I saw a string of pariah dogs without an ounce of hair on some of them . . . plunge in and refresh themselves very comfortably.' The pictures of elegant eighteenth-century Calcutta, city of palaces, do not tell us of this side of life.

The elaborate architecture of Calcutta gave the impression of Grecian temples, 'with great projecting porticoes, or surrounded by colonnades or arcades'. But here is a more piercing eighteenth-century eye:

> The quarter inhabited by the English . . . laid off in regular wide streets with spacious and showy houses, such as in appearance eclipse, (not to speak of London) almost anything in Paris and Italy. I say in appearance for they will not bear an examination, they are all of brick plastered over and whitewashed, but all attempt some order of architecture and you see nothing but portico's, columnades, galleries, etc. etc., some few in good taste, several tolerable and many more wretchedly bad.

Bengal became the first large area on mainland Asia to be subjugated by the British, and so from the beginning Calcutta, the centre of Bengal administration, was the East India Company's most important city. Bengal itself was described by a Scot who served there in the eighteenth century as one of 'the richest, most populous and best cultivated kingdoms of the world'. Every early traveller agreed with him; and the Mughals (rather oddly for them) described it as 'the paradise of the earth'. Bengal mainly consists of flat alluvial plain, watered by two great rivers; much of the land is extremely fertile. Transport by river was easy, and this obviously had great significance for British traders collecting goods of all sorts from a large area.

The most important and the most valuable of these goods were textiles – cotton and silk. Huge amounts of cotton piece-goods were woven during the seventeenth and eighteenth centuries. For instance, at Dacca in 1776 it was said that 25,000 weavers produced 180,000 pieces of cloth from thread spun by 80,000 women. Because this cloth was of a high quality and very cheap, there was a great demand for it in Europe. Indian textiles, especially the painted and resist-dyed cottons known as 'chintzes' (after the Indian word *chint* meaning 'variegated'), were far superior to the dyed fabrics then produced in Europe and were greatly admired by the English for their clear, lovely colours and for the fact that they could withstand repeated washing. However, it was found that the traditional Indian patterns were too alien for mass European taste, so sample western patterns were sent out from Great Britain and the Netherlands to be copied. But of course the Indian artist seldom copied exactly, and the result was a style much influenced by European decorative conventions yet very Indian and exotic in its total impact. In trading terms it was a sensational success, and very large shipments of chintz were sent to Europe in the form of bedspreads, wall-hangings and dress-materials. One can see the effects of the influence these had in much modern floral fabric design; one cannot imagine what design development in the West would have been like without this powerful Indian influence.

Other valuable goods came from Bengal: to Europe were sent indigo and saltpetre (for use in gunpowder); rice, sugar cane and tobacco were grown and exported by Company officials all over the middle and far East; and, finally, opium from poppies, which the Company exported mainly to China in return for that other valuable commodity, tea. (Cultivation of opium poppies was not legal in those days in China, and the East India Company had a monopoly of supply.)

The East India Company, faced with complex and lucrative trade on the one hand and constant troubles of one sort or another with the Mughal Empire on the other, might well have discovered quite early on that it had taken on too much to handle efficiently. As it was, by the time the Company found this to be true, it was so deeply dug into India that the British government could take it over without difficulty. From the beginning the Company had a fixed and workable structure, an important factor in the later growth of the Indian Civil Service. A system of ranks was established: a man began serving for five

Looms used in the manufacture of cotton rugs, a drawing by William Simpson, 1861.

years as a Writer, and the minimum age for a Writer to come out from England was sixteen. These Writers were really human xerox-machines and have left behind them 48,000 volumes of records covering the Company's 250 years of official existence! (This unique record of documentation is in the India Office Library and Records in London.) Five years as a Writer at £5 per annum were followed by three years as a Factor at £15 per annum, then three years as a Junior Merchant (£30 per annum). After this followed the highest rank, the Senior Merchant at £40 a year, with a special salary of £300 for the Governors of Bombay, Madras and Calcutta. These miserable salaries were supplemented by various small allowances but even so did not begin to cover the average man's expenses, particularly if he had a wife and family out in India with him.

How did the English merchants manage? Luckily, quite early on it became clear to the Directors in London that freedom of trade, which had at first been frowned on, would allow the Company's servants to make fortunes which cost the Company nothing, and at the same time would turn the small English settlements into thriving ports. Successful private trade would make the

Mid-eighteenth-century hanging of painted and dyed cotton from the Coromandel coast, northern Madras. The design is adapted from an engraving in the Don Quixote series by Bonnart.

Detail of a petticoat border of painted and dyed cotton, probably made under Dutch patronage on the Coromandel coast, southern Madras, in the late eighteenth century.

English ports 'great and famous', wrote the Directors in 1717: 'We shall always be glad when trade flourishes in India, as well for the opportunity it affords our servants to get estates honestly, as that our own settlements are bettered thereby.'

Local or 'country' trading up and down the coasts was extremely lucrative though full of risks: piracy and storms decimated ships. Profit margins were very high: for instance 75 per cent was thought to be a fair estimate in the 1760s for profits on dealing in salt and tobacco. British ships carrying goods to Persia reckoned to make between 50 and 80 per cent. No wonder in successful seasons large fortunes were made very quickly. In India, few men were able to accumulate wealth slowly; they either made money quickly or lost everything. Those who did become very rich returned to England, built themselves large country houses and began, to the envious annoyance of the stay-at-homes, a life of luxury far higher up the social ladder than they had been before they left for India. These 'nabobs', who often entered Parliament, caught the public imagination. Robert Clive was the most outstanding among them: he made the biggest fortune to come out of Bengal in the eighteenth century.

European overseer watching irrigation work in progress, 1785. Women then as now did much of the carrying of rubble and earth in construction work.

Clive first arrived in India in 1744 at the age of seventeen with no money to speak of and returned to England at the age of twenty-eight, famous after his success at the Battle of Plassey (1757) with his first huge fortune. (He was to return later to India and make another.) Clive was a merchant and a soldier, successful at both. He made much of his money in private trading ventures, but he also received large 'presents' of money from local rulers in thanks for services rendered. Later he was heavily criticized by the British government for this, but he and all other Company officials defended themselves by saying that presents were permissible as long as they were a voluntary offering made for genuine services done in the course of duty and did no damage to the Company's interest. A *lakh* of rupees (about £11,000) was a standard large 'present' from a Mughal ruler – and the giving of presents was a habitual part of Mughal life. After Plassey, presents worth £1,238,575 were distributed to various Englishmen, and Clive himself received over sixteen *lakhs*. Grateful rulers gave these large sums in thanks for British protection, or indeed for putting them on the throne and helping to keep them there.

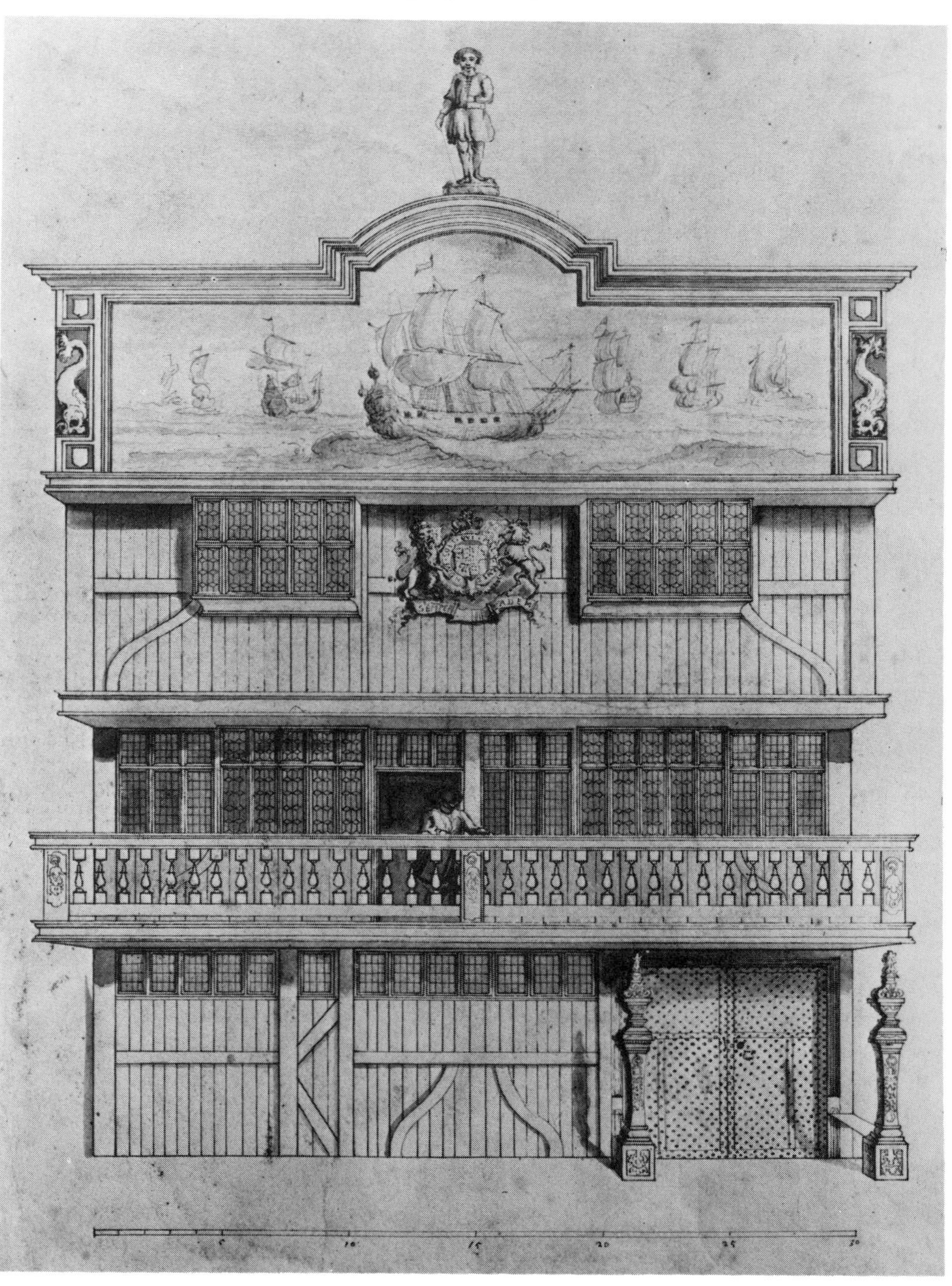

East India House, Leadenhall Street, London in about 1711. This was the Jacobean house leased to the Company in 1661. The house was rebuilt in 1726 and again in 1799.

East India House, Leadenhall Street, rebuilt in 1799 by Richard Tupp and Henry Holland. It was here that in 1801 the Company's library was founded and the unique collection of drawings and prints (of which this view is one) was begun.

There is no doubt that corruption grew common amongst Company officials in the eighteenth century. Official pay being so low, and chances of exploitation of the natives so great, it was a very exceptional man who put the Company's interests before his own. This was true of Englishmen of every rank. Even the newly-arrived teenage Writer could not hope to live on £5 per annum in the extravagant, hard-gambling, heavy-drinking society of the eighteenth century. For instance, it was reported that in Madras in 1762 few gentlemen spent less than £5000 to £6000 a year, and the Governor lived at a rate of £20,000. It was a mad world of luxury and acquisitiveness, and Clive himself, knowing it only too well from the inside, began the struggle to modify some of the worst abuses. Warren Hastings continued the process of reform, but it was Lord Cornwallis, Governor-General from 1786 to 1793, who finished the job of putting the Company's affairs in order.

Robert Clive, 1st Lord Clive (1725-74), a replica of a portrait by Matthew Neil Dance. In 1744 Clive entered the service of the East India Company as a clerk. He then became an ensign in the army and spent much of the next sixteen years fighting the French. Following his famous victory at Plassey in 1757, Clive was appointed Governor of Bengal. His career was highly successful and larded with official honours, yet at the end of his life his actions in India were criticized and subjected to a government inquiry. He eventually committed suicide; his depression was probably exacerbated by the opium he took to alleviate his ill health.

By 1784 the East India Company had debts of £8 million; it was becoming painfully clear that without support from the government it might well cease to exist. Pitt's India Act of 1784 gave Parliament control over the Company; a Governor-General was appointed to supervise the Presidencies of Madras, Bombay and Calcutta. Trade was still the main concern. William Pitt the Younger knew that most of the Company's debts had come about because of territorial entanglements; he made it clear that he hoped these would cease:

> The first and principal object would be to take care to prevent the Government from being ambitious and bent on conquest. Propensities of that nature had already involved India in great expenses, and cost much bloodshed. These, therefore, ought most studiously to be avoided. Commerce was our object, and with a view to its extension, a pacific system should prevail, and a system of defence and conciliation.

Portrait by a Lucknow artist from about 1815 of Tilly Kettle painting a portrait of Shuja-ad-daula. The painting is undoubtedly based on an original by Kettle, now lost. Tilly Kettle (1735-89) was the first British portrait painter to venture to India, where he spent the years 1769 to 1776. He was in Oudh under the patronage of the Nawab Shuja-ad-daula, who is seen here with the heir apparent and nine of his younger brothers. Other professional British artists who went to India were Thomas and William Daniell, who arrived in 1786, Johann Zoffany (1783), George Chinnery (1802) and Edward Lear (1874).

There was no mention in the Act about moral duty of the rights of the governed. A sense of responsibility for the condition of India was yet to grow in Parliament. Pitt's 'pacific system', like Roe's 'quiet trade', with no aggression and no political involvement, was a capitalist dream, with no basis in reality.

The Company's part in Indian politics was not over at all: it was in fact about to grow rapidly. The collapse of the Mughal empire during the eighteenth century meant that the British were increasingly involved with local rulers at odds with each other. They found that they could not isolate trade from political commitments. Quite the opposite: in order to safeguard and promote trade they had to continue to exert military and political power in the many troubled areas throughout the Mughal kingdom.

At first the British, still hoping for power without responsibility, had instituted a dual system of government in the areas under their control; the Company was titular *diwan* (governor), but practical authority was delegated to the local rulers. This was disastrous; the decaying Mughal Empire produced officials whose idea of government was tyranny and greed. An English Resident wrote in 1769:

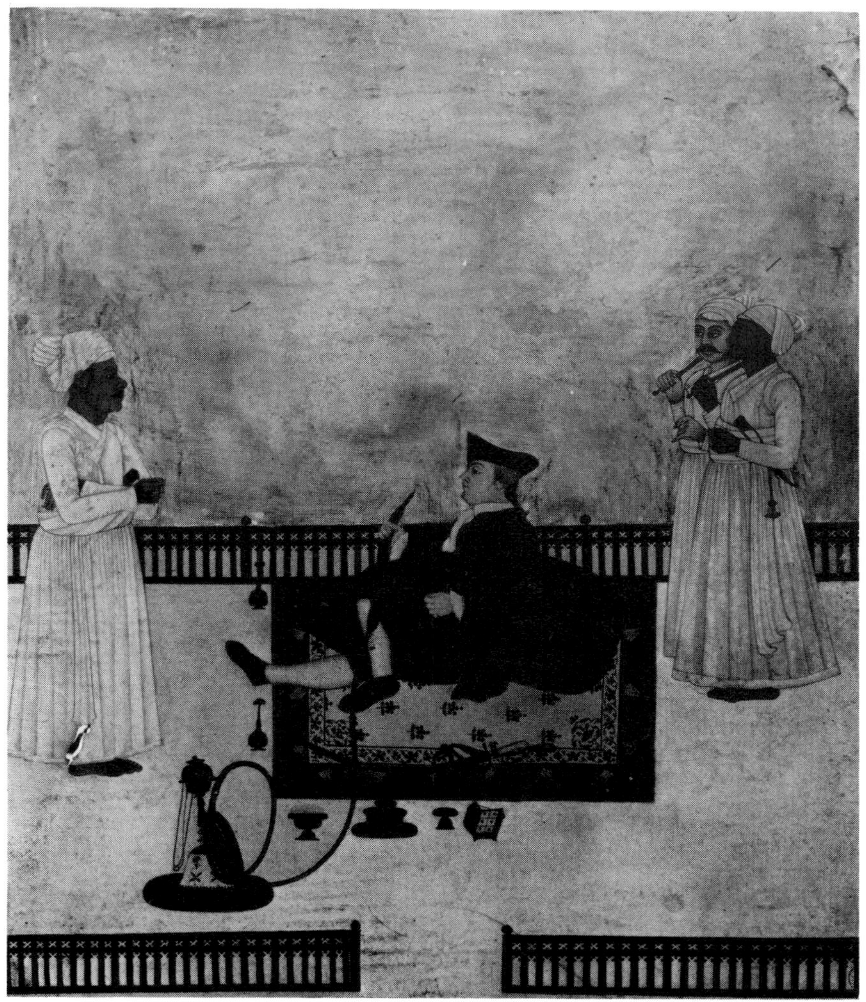

An official of the East India Company, perhaps the Surgeon William Fullarton, on a terrace smoking a *hookah* and talking to a visitor. His servants hold fly switches. Fullarton practised as a surgeon in Bengal and Bihar from 1744 until about 1766. He made a collection of Indian paintings.

The Bengal Levee, an etching by James Gillray from an original drawing done on the spot by an amateur, 1792. The scene is a reception held by Lord Cornwallis in Old Government House during his first period as Governor (1786-93). Cornwallis is in the doorway. Many other Calcutta figures are shown. On the far right, for example, Mr J. Miller of the Police is having shady dealings with Robert MacFarlane, Clerk of the Market.

Since the accession of the company to the Diwani the condition of the people of this country has been worse than it was before. . . . This fine country, which flourished under the most despotic and arbitrary government [the Mughals] is verging towards ruin.

Things could not go on like this; the dual system was discontinued and the Company took over practical authority as well. This meant that the numbers of civilians and military supported by the Company had to grow to cope with all the extra work; and with this extra financial burden it was no wonder that the Company was bankrupt. The India trade had also been falling off each

year and was lost in 1813, except for tea and the production of opium in Bengal, which remained a government monopoly. The industrial revolution caused English cotton to become plentiful and cheap, so that by 1818 there was no demand for Indian cotton in England. Those busy weavers in Dacca described earlier were now idle; here is Charles Edward Trevelyan's description of what happened:

> The peculiar kind of silky cotton formerly grown in Bengal, from which fine Dacca muslims used to be made, was hardly ever seen; the population of the town of Dacca has fallen from 150,000 to 30,000 or 40,000. . . . The only cotton manufacturers which stand their ground in India are of the very coarse kind and English cotton manufactures are generally consumed by all above the very poorest throughout India. . . . Dacca, which was the Manchester of India, has fallen off from a very flourishing town to a very poor and small one.

So the commercial side of the Company was increasingly unprofitable; but on the political side administrative improvements came quickly after the arrival of Lord Cornwallis in 1783 as Governor-General. The days of the trading buccaneer and the oppressor were over.

Warren Hastings had already begun the process of political consolidation; without him British India could hardly have survived. Cornwallis was almost as important; he cleaned up the administration so that it never went back to the old corruption. He laid the foundations of the great civil service tradition which was at the heart of the British Raj. Also, because of his disapproval of oriental ways of behaving and thinking, he took all power away from Indians and introduced a completely anglicized power-structure. He applied an English philosophy of government regardless of whether it fitted the Indian peasant or not, and it often did not. Luckily, as we shall see in the next chapter, many Englishmen who knew India well opposed some of his reforms, effective compromises were introduced and a balance was struck instead. Cornwallis was a practical man of integrity and common sense who lacked vision. Hastings had vision as well as a sensitive response to the real India; he knew Persian, took a great interest in its literature and poetry; he founded an Arabic college in Calcutta and encouraged the first translation of the *Bhagavad Gita*. India has always had Englishmen like Hastings to balance those like Cornwallis, and such variety in its servants was one of the great strengths of the Raj.

The year 1818 is an important one in the history of British India: 'in that year the British dominion *in* India became the British dominion *of* India,' as Spear says. India was an entity again, externally and politically at any rate. One area after another came under British rule: an estimate published at the time said that the East India Company controlled 553,000 square miles with a probable population of 87,000,000, while its allies and tributary chiefs controlled an additional 590,000 square miles and 43 million people; still independent were a mere 127,000 square miles containing 6 million people. This was a far cry from the day when the total English civilian population of, for example, Madras was only 114 (in 1700), comprising twenty-seven Company's

Warren Hastings (1732-1818). Warren Hastings entered the service of the East India Company in 1750 and by 1772 had become Governor-General of Bengal. His judicial and administrative reforms as Governor-General of India restored the Company after a period of corruption and near bankruptcy. Eventually he was recalled from India and was himself accused of corruption and impeached in 1788. He was acquitted after a trial lasting 145 days over a period of seven years.

servants, twenty-nine freemen (unattached traders), thirty-nine sailors, eleven widows and eight maidens, out of a total population of only 300,000, none of whom would have considered themselves under British domination.

In 1834 came the end of the Company as a trading organization. By an Act of Parliament, it lost its commercial side and became solely the agency through which the British governed India. It was a civil service with a trading company's name. Then, after the rebellion in 1857 (the Indian Mutiny), the East India Company's civil power was taken over directly by the British government, and the Company died. The name with all its exotic associations became a memory, kept from fading completely by place names like London's East India Docks. The extraordinary growth of a merchant venture into a civil service controlling an empire was complete; the Company's Raj was over.

3 Paragons of Vision

India was 'the one sphere in which an Englishman who is neither born in the purple nor minded to flatter mobs, can hope just at present to serve his country to any serious purpose,' said Sir James Stephen, who held high office in India, in 1876. He was impressed by the efficiency and integrity of the Indian Civil Service, and indeed, by the time the British government took it over from the East India Company, it was an extremely efficient machine: flexible, decentralized, personal in the best sense, with a superstructure of just, incorrupt bureaucracy.

This system of civil government had grown naturally out of the Company's structure. Young Writers going out to India tended to specialize and would either join the commercial department or choose the administrative side and become revenue collectors, magistrates etc. By the late eighteenth century, Company civilians were paid an adequate salary at last, to discourage corruption. Their role in India became increasingly complex as the responsibilities of empire grew.

By great good luck, there were men of quite exceptional ability working in India during the crucial years of development and modification at the end of the eighteenth and the beginning of the nineteenth centuries. There had been giants before, like Clive and Hastings; but without a brilliant group of four men, Thomas Munro, Mountstuart Elphinstone, John Malcolm and Charles Metcalfe, the Indian Civil Service would certainly have developed differently and might not have become the excellent system it undoubtedly was.

These paragons of vision knew India well and understood her problems; they energetically resisted Lord Cornwallis' effort to impose British constitutional principles on India. Cornwallis' 'new order of things', though it contained much that was good, included re-division of a civilian's duties into neat compartments and an impersonal centralized government which imposed English ideas and institutions on to Indian society willy-nilly. Munro, Elphinstone, Malcolm and Metcalfe, a group of friends whose areas of service covered the South, Central Deccan, the West coast and the North of India, were all of the same mind; they felt that the British government was bent on destroying the India they loved in the interests of bureaucratic efficiency. They knew that the only effective way for the British to control rural India was through a paternalistic system, with one man responsible for the whole of the peasant's welfare –

Sir Thomas Munro (1761-1827). He arrived in India in 1780 as a soldier and later switched back and forth between military and civil duties, finally settling in the latter. His knowledge and understanding of all aspects of Indian affairs were second to none. He became Governor of Madras in 1819 and after an active and highly successful governorship died of cholera on tour. His death was mourned as a public calamity by all classes of the community.

Mountstuart Elphinstone (1779-1859). Elphinstone arrived in Calcutta in 1796 with an appointment in the Bengal Civil Service. He went to Fort William College (newly opened) in 1801 and then, after service in Cabul, became Resident at Poona in 1810. While he was at Poona all his property and beloved books were destroyed when the residency was burnt down in the wars against the Mahrattas. As Governor of Bombay from 1819 to 1827, he prepared a complex code of laws and laid down a system of public education. He left India in 1827 and spent his retirement writing his *History of India*.

for the settlement and collection of his taxes and the solving of his legal problems. They were angry because Cornwallis separated the jobs of Collector and Magistrate, thereby increasing red tape and decreasing effectiveness. They wanted a personal, human and tangible form of government, something the *ryot* (peasant) could understand and get at. Cornwallis' new system was already established in Bengal, but because of the efforts of Munro and his friends South, West and North India eventually adopted the personalized system, with the Collector in charge of both revenue and justice.

Thomas Munro arrived in India at the age of nineteen as a soldier and later became a civilian; he hid a poetic and sensitive nature under a bluff soldier's exterior. His first big appointment was to assist in the settlement of the land in the South of India ceded by Tipu Sultan in 1792; he belived with all his heart in the 'noble peasant' and felt that one of his priorities should be a fair system of land settlement and revenue. He wrote vividly to his sister describing this hard work:

From daybreak till eleven or twelve at night I am never alone except at meals and these *altogether* do not take up an hour. I am pressed on the one hand by the settlements of the revenue and on the other by the investigation of murders, robberies, and all the evils which have arisen from the long course of profligate and tyrannical government. Living in a tent, there is no escaping for a few hours from the crowd; there is no locking oneself up on pretence of more important business, as a man might do in a house.

His aims were to gain the peasant his own land, to guide him with paternal and simple government, and so to avoid the inappropriate artificialities of a sophisticated European type of rule. He was against innovation for its own sake:

Sir John Malcolm (1769-1833). When interviewed by the directors of the East India Company, the young Scottish boy said in answer to the question, 'What would you do if you met Hyder Ali?': 'Cut off his heid.' Malcolm arrived in India in 1783 as an ensign and was an energetic soldier. In 1798 he joined the diplomatic service under Wellesley and became an expert in Persian affairs. He hoped after a full diplomatic and military life in India to become Governor, but Elphinstone got the post; he then expected to become Lieutenant-Governor of Central India, but Munro was appointed instead. He eventually became Governor of Bombay in 1827 and left India in 1830.

Sir Charles Metcalfe (1785-1846). Charles Theophilus Metcalfe was the son of a former major in the Bengal Army. He became Resident at Delhi in 1811 and Resident and Civil Commissioner in the Delhi territories in 1825. In 1833 he acted as Governor-General between the departure of Lord Bentinck and the arrival of Lord Auckland and his sisters Emily and Fanny Eden. Metcalfe left India in 1838, became Governor of Jamaica in 1839 and Governor of Canada in 1843. He died in England in 1846.

The ruling vice of our government is innovation, . . . it is time that we should learn that neither the face of the country, its property, nor its society, are things that can be suddenly improved by any contrivance of ours, though they may be greatly injured by what we mean for their good.

He also spoke angrily against red tape: 'It is too much regulation that ruins everything. Englishmen suppose no country can be saved without English institutions.' His liberal-mindedness had a great effect on his contemporaries; in a country like India they could see the force of his belief that a personal government from tent and saddle would achieve far more than distant direction from an office. It was becoming standard practice at the beginning of the nineteenth century to tour one's area under canvas, and with this development the efficiency of the civil service system increased dramatically. It was often uncomfortable; tents could get blown down or flooded and, as Munro found, were no use for privacy, but most Englishmen serving in India loved being on tour and would have echoed the delight in camping felt by Philip Woodruff, who himself was a District Officer in the twentieth century:

The first sniff of wet straw from the floor of the canvas bathroom behind the tent; the first sip of smoky tea; the kiss of the pillow on your cheek, cooler than in a bungalow and perhaps slightly moist with dew; above all, the first morning ride from camp with the scent of sugar-cane cooking at the corner of the field, the tops of the tall feathery grass still silver with dew – one by one each remembered scent and sound peeled away one layer of sweaty saline incrustation, the deposit of eight months of irritated wrangling and intrigue. Within three or four days, you were a different man. The people of your district were no longer cases to be got through, no longer tiresome creatures always making work by their absurd inability to agree. They turned suddenly into human beings who would squat on the ground and tell you their troubles, people childish no doubt, cunning but simple, laughable, stubborn, affectionate people, callous and gentle, cruel and compassionate, people for whom you too felt a real affection as you sat on a string cot in the village street and drank buffalo milk in which sugar had been stirred by a dirty finger. It was an affection that would survive the next hot weather, though it might lie dormant, aestivating beneath the parched and dusty surface of the sun-baked soil. It was from camp, not from Indian mistresses, that some of the English learnt what India was like.

Thomas Munro would have agreed heartily with that. He had a huge area of India to cover and spent a large part of his time camping and touring. He was an impressive man with a boundless energy for work. His friend Elphinstone has left us this description of him, of his

strong practical good sense, his simplicity and frankness, his perfect good humour, his real benevolence . . . his activity and his truthfulness of mind, easily pleased with anything and delighted with those things that in general have no effect but on a youthful imagination. The effect of these last qualities is heightened by their contrast with his stern countenance and searching eye.

Munro knew several Indian languages well and as a result understood and sympathized with his subjects. He hated those English who belived that they were intrinsically superior to the Indian: 'Foreign conquerors', he wrote, 'have treated the natives with violence and often with great cruelty, but none has

Durbar of the Emperor Akbar II, with his four sons and Archibald Seton, the British Resident at Delhi, *c.* 1806. Akbar II was a weak Emperor ruled by his women, but Seton (who preceded Charles Metcalfe as Resident) dealt with him diplomatically and kept his friendship. The portraits here are closely observed.

treated them with so much scorn as we, none has stigmatized the whole people as unworthy of trust.' Bishop Heber, while Bishop of Calcutta during the same period, travelled all over India and spoke ruefully of the 'foolish, surly national pride' of the British: 'We shut out the natives from our society and a bullying insolent manner is continually assumed in speaking to them.'

In such a mixed company of civilians, it is clear how important were the humane and far-sighted views of Munro, Elphinstone, Malcolm and Metcalfe. They believed that one day Indians should govern themselves; they saw the danger as well as the strength in Lord Wellesley's assertion that 'I can declare my conscientious conviction that no greater blessing can be conferred on the

Richard, 1st Marquess of Wellesley and Earl of Mornington (1760-1842), Governor-General of India from 1798 to 1805. Wellesley's main aim was to maintain British supremacy in India, which was threatened by France, the rival trading power, and her allies, such as Tipu of Mysore. Tipu was defeated in 1799 and the British position in Mysore safeguarded. By supporting local governments with a system of subsidiary alliances, Wellesley made the provinces of Tanjore, the Carnatic, Oudh and Hyderabad safe for British interests. Eventually Wellesley's extravagance and his aggressive policies so provoked the directors of the East India Company that he was recalled in 1805.

native inhabitants of India than the extension of the British authority, influence and power.'

But they also believed wholeheartedly in the work they were doing; they never had any doubts that their duties were right and God-given. The importance of the Christian faith and ethic to the men who ruled India should never be overlooked or made light of; though the Victorians were to take their crusading zeal too far, there is no doubt at all that one of the main reasons why the British Empire was as great as it was lies in its backbone of a deeply-rooted Christian moral outlook with its emphasis on serving others without thought of personal gain.

Mountstuart Elphinstone's Christianity was not in the least dogmatic; he belonged to the rational eighteenth century, and he felt that only by education and example would the Indians see, as he put it, the 'obvious superiority of Christianity'. But 'to the mixture of religion . . . with our plans . . . I must strongly object.' No dogmatic teaching: the country's civil and judicial problems came first.

Elphinstone was a most attractive personality: an all-rounder of great intelligence and vision, humour and sympathy, highly educated and passionately fond of reading, but fond too of physical relaxation – pig-sticking particularly. He was the perfect scholar-statesman, a man of action with a thirst for intellectual pursuits – for Latin, Greek and Persian classics and for history, philosophy and law. The following entry in his diary illustrates the balance in his life: while fighting in a campaign, after a specially active engagement, he wrote: 'I breakfasted with Kennedy and talked about Hafiz, Saadi [Persian poets], Horace, and Anacreon. At nine I left him and went to the trenches.' When a particular thorn in his flesh who had taken up a lot of his time was finally brought to justice and imprisoned, Elphinstone's comment was: 'Now I have time to read Cicero in the mornings.' He says endearingly of himself: 'I have enjoyed – I mean relished – society and study and business and action and adventure, all according to their several natures.'

The Marquess of Wellesley and his party view an elephant fight while breakfasting with the Nabob of Oudh, 1813.

Elphinstone served in the South and West of India, ending up as Governor of Bombay from 1819 to 1827. In the period immediately before he became Governor he toured and camped through the Deccan area as thoroughly as Munro did; indeed when he left the Deccan for Bombay he said ruefully, 'I sighed for my tent and its compact equipment and the fine climate we have left.' He knew his India well, present and past; he wrote a history of India and a history of the Kingdom of Cabul, both of which were long standard works.

John Malcolm found time to write even more books in his busy active life. He started out as a roughly-educated soldier, having joined the Company's service at the age of fourteen, but his own drive for self-completion transformed him into a finished statesman, scholar and writer. He wrote a *History of Persia* (still regarded as a standard work), a *Political History of India*, a book about Central India and another about its government, a *Life* of Clive, as well as some verse and a collection of Persian fairy tales. He had super-abundant energy, and like the other three men in this group wanted to preserve Indian society in all its variety. All four men felt that the British government was bent on sweeping

Haileybury College, for fifty years the training centre for East India Company servants. Designed by William Wilkins, Haileybury was opened in 1809 (from 1806 students had been temporarily housed in Hertford Castle). In January 1858 the College was closed and the buildings remained empty until the present school opened in 1862. Wilkins' design played an important part in the development of the college campus.

away the old India they loved. Brisk efficient civilians straight out from England, full of abstract principles and bureaucracy, filled Malcolm with horror; he said he dreaded more than anyone

> an able Calcutta civilian, whose travels are limited to two or three hundred miles, with a hookah in his mouth, some good but abstract maxims in his head, the Regulations in his right hand, the Company's Charter in his left, and a quire of foolscap before him.

Charles Metcalfe was the most successful and influential in India of all these men; his area of influence was in the North, in the Delhi area. He arrived in India fresh from Eton; by twenty-seven he was Resident at Delhi, virtually Governor of that large area. His rule was most enlightened: indeed in his penal theory he was a century ahead of his time anywhere. He disliked the death penalty and discontinued it; he stopped flogging, because he did not believe in the vindictive aspect of punishment. He forbade the slave trade and the burning of widows (*sati*, the obligatory immolation of a Hindu widow on her husband's pyre, was still common); he collected swords and spears, beat them literally into ploughshares, and returned them to the owners. He saw always with great clarity and realism the British role in India: that the British should eradicate anarchy and misrule but not expect permanent gratitude for this necessary service once the Indian memory of anarchy had faded.

Our dominion in India is by conquest; it is naturally disgusting to the inhabitants and can only be maintained by military force. It is our positive duty to render them justice, to respect and protect their rights, and to study their happiness. By the performance of this duty we may allay and keep dormant their innate disaffection.

He was liberal and realistic; he rose through the Civil Service until he became acting Governor-General. But his liberal views had by this time annoyed the conservative Court of Directors of the Company in London and he got no further in India. He resigned and ended up as Governor-General of Canada. This departure was a great loss to India, particularly because the next Governor-General, Lord Auckland, involved India in the utterly disastrous Afghan wars, a move that Metcalfe, with his realistic knowledge of India, would never have

South side of the Quadrangle, Haileybury, *c.* 1855, one of eight beautiful drawings done anonymously and presented to the India Office in 1855.

John Beames (1837-1902). He arrived in India fresh from Haileybury in 1858 and left in 1893. This photograph must have been taken not long after his arrival. He soon began to grow a beard because, as he says in his memoirs, of the tedium of shaving and remained bearded thereafter.

made. He must have agreed wholeheartedly with this letter written to him by Elphinstone about the nature of their Empire:

I used to think our Empire made of glass but when one considers the rough usage it has stood both in old times and recent, one is apt to think it is made of iron. I believe it is of steel which cuts through everything if you carry the edge even, but is very apt to snap short if it falls into unskilful hands.

'Unskilful hands' were common in India because men came out so young, their education cut short. Lord Wellesley, Governor-General from 1798 to 1805, saw the value of men like Thomas Munro and felt it was imperative that all aspiring young civil servants should have extra education specially geared to their job in India, so that standards would not fall too far below those of an equivalent university education. Wellesley knew the need for quality:

The Empire must be considered as a sacred trust and a permanent possession. Duty, policy and honour require that it should not be administered as a temporary and precarious acquisition.

He realized that men who educated themselves as Malcolm had done were unusual; most of the young men who came out went callow to their isolated districts, where callow they remained. To ensure that this new Empire was run by men to suit it, Wellesley founded Fort William College in Calcutta to educate them; every young man was to spend three years there, where he would learn Indian history, law and oriental languages and general subjects like philosophy,

Sketch by John Beames of his wife Ellen asleep entitled *Floating down the Chelum River. Feb. 7th 1861*. Beames became engaged to Ellen Geary before he left for India. She followed him out later and in 1859 they married. This sketch was done when the young couple moved from Gujrat to Ambala; Ellen, who had already had one miscarriage, is pregnant again. (The baby, a boy, was born on 14 May and died eight days later.)

Sketch by John Beames of his bungalow (the word is taken from the Hindi *bungla* – country) in Chittagong. Beames was Commissioner and Judge at Chittagong in 1878 and 1879. He wrote of his home in a letter: 'As we sit here in a verandah hung with orchids in bloom we look down on masses of palms and other trees . . . the great white river full of ships beyond, and over the long line of trees we can see the faint blue line of the sea.' But the Beames hated Chittagong: 'I have never seen so lovely a place to look at, nor one so loathesome to live in. . . . We were supremely unhappy at Chittagong. In fact we spent there two of the most miserable years of our existence.'

ethics and world history. Fort William College was in working order, and the first young men, who included the brilliant Charles Metcalfe, were being taught, when the Company's Directors in London first heard about it. Enraged, they refused to sanction this extra financial burden. Equally enraged, Wellesley argued that his college would build up corporate spirit and pride in the service and benefit the Empire. The Court of Directors demolished the arguments for a college in India but instead commited themselves to founding one in England. 'The East India College, Herts.' opened in 1806 and moved to Haileybury in 1809; it lasted for fifty years. It ended not because it was useless but because a new system of open competitive examination was introduced by the British government, raising standards even higher.

Haileybury was like an Oxford or Cambridge college, where men learnt oriental languages, classics, mathematics and general and Indian law; emphasis was put on political economy and world history, then hardly taught at the

A gentleman in his private office, 1813. The *duftoree* is refilling the inkpot.

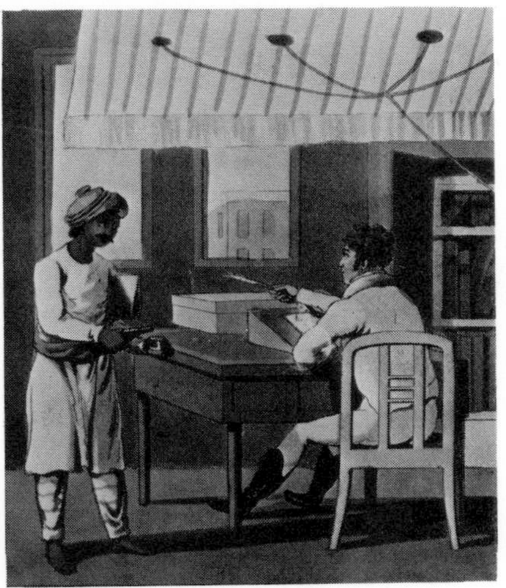

older universities. The staff included men of such eminence as Malthus and Sir James Stephen. From contemporary descriptions by young men who went there, it seems that Haileybury's aims were sometimes higher than its achievements. John Beames, a student in 1857 just before the college closed, said that it was 'considered bad form to talk about India or to allude to the fact that we were going there soon'. He tells us about the single occasion in his experience when a lecturer actually dealt with life in India:

> Sir James Stephen . . . pulled out of his pocket a letter he had just received from a Civilian in the North-West Provinces and with his eyes half-shut in his pearls-before-swine manner, read it to us. In his letter the writer described his daily life and the style of work which we were shortly to enter on. It interested me deeply, but I found that by my fellows it was regarded simply as an expedient of 'Old Jimmy's' for shirking a lecture and merely valuable because it gave us one lecture less to take notes.

There is no doubt that, though Haileybury's success was a mixed one, it had the effect of raising standards during the crucial first half of the nineteenth century when the Raj was expanding and consolidating its powers and characteristics. The best argument in favour of Haileybury was that it fostered unity of interest – 'team spirit'; because of Haileybury, India was administered by men who knew each other and were inspired by the same ideals of honour and duty; they worked not for themselves but for India, with, in Beames' words, the 'sure and simple maxim that we are bound to govern India in trust for the natives and for India itself'. They were often tough, manly philistines; they believed in Hard Work, independence of spirit and the need to take decisions without hesitating.

A Punjab Court Room, painting by A. F. P. Harcourt. Harcourt served with the Bengal Infantry from 1855 to 1859; he was with the 30th Native Infantry when they mutinied in 1857 and in 1858 took part in the relief of Lucknow.

Model dating from the first half of the nineteenth century of a *cutcherry* court, presided over by an East India Company official called the *zamindar*.

'Governing men is grand work,' wrote John Beames enthusiastically,

> the noblest of all occupations though perhaps the most difficult, and as I acquired by degrees more experience and greater familiarity with those petty but indispensable matters of routine which hang about all work, I began to feel my strength and enjoy my duties more and more.

John Beames, who describes himself as an 'ordinary average Englishman' living in Victoria's reign, served in India for twenty-five years after his stint at Haileybury. He was in many ways not ordinary at all, because he has left us a remarkably good picture of life in India in his *Memoirs of a Bengal Civilian*, published for the first time only in 1961. He is a true writer, with a natural eye for detail and an expressive style; these memoirs give a most vivid impression of what it was like to live and work in India in the last half of the nineteenth century. Beames also found time to study Indian philology and to write two large works on Indian languages (*Outlines of Indian Philology* and a three-volume *Comparative Grammar of Modern Aryan Languages in India*), both of which remained standard textbooks for many years.

Beames was too outspoken to rise very high in the Indian Civil Service; he had a quick temper and a caustic tongue which his superiors found uncomfortable. He was posted to a wide variety of places all over the Punjab and Bengal. His twenty-five years were very typical: as district officer and magistrate and

Chur Case – Local Inquiry, an example of local justice at work, 1896.

collector, judge and commissioner, his work included every possible variation from deposing Rajas to settling a *ryot's* family dispute; from providing food for the British army as it passed through his province (he was very caustic about the generals and their confusions) to himself being feasted by hill tribesmen, when he, his wife and children

all sat down in rows, and neat little stools of plaited bamboo with a plantain leaf carefully folded on the top were placed before each person. Cups made of a length of bamboo cut off slanting were given to us, and a man came round and filled them with rum and water from an earthen jar. Then we all drank. This, it seems, is an indispensable preliminary, after which the plantain leaves were unfolded and revealed a mess of eggs, rice, fowl, chillies, etc., all very nicely cooked. The Mughs are celebrated for their cookery.

(This is a fact that all English families in India knew, and the Mughs, a tribe from the Burmese border, were found in every possible kitchen.) This visit to the Mughs took place while Beames was commissioner and judge at Chittagong. His descriptions of the scenery show how perceptive his eye was:

Then you come to the hills, and the river, broad, rapid and deep, swirls in eddies of dark green water round the base of sandstone cliffs topped and tufted with palm, mango, bamboo and other trees all laced with giant creepers gorgeously coloured. In one place a whole rock face fifty or sixty feet high is one blaze of red, another of yellow; a little further on an immense Beaumontia with its great white trumpet-shaped flowers covers half the hillside. Every ledge and cranny is full of orchids,

The Emperor Akbar holding a hunting circle. Akbar (1542-1602) ruled from 1556 to 1605. His splendid harem is in the background, guarded by a eunuch.

The Emperor Jahangir (1569-1627, ruled 1605-27) receiving a prince.

The Emperor Shah Jehan (1592-1666, ruled 1627-58). He was the greatest builder of the Mughal Emperors, his best known building being the Taj Mahal, a monument to his beloved wife Mumtaz Mahal. This portrait is inscribed 'A good portrait of me in my 40th year, the work of Bichitr'.

A Dust Whirlwind in the Plains, painting by William Simpson (1823-99).

Painting of a pile-carpet loom at Munsur (Mysore) by a South Indian artist, *c.* 1850. This picture was presented to the East India Company's Museum in 1850 and may well have accompanied a specimen carpet for the Museum. It is typical of the 'Company' paintings produced under British patronage. Indian artists were commissioned to paint sets of subjects – trades, transport, servants etc. Their works were collected as souvenirs of life in India. The coming of the camera killed this style of painting.

Gouache by a Murshidabad artist, *c.* 1775-80, of a European officer standing under a tree by a river, with his servant and dog. This was evidently a portrait of a particular individual, whose identity is now lost.

My Tents, 1840, a watercolour by J. B. Bellasis depicting a survey officer in camp.

Government House, Calcutta, from the east. When the Marquess of Wellesley became Governor-General in 1798, he immediately started to plan this new Government House, finding the existing buildings inadequate and lacking in dignity. The building was based on the design of Kedleston Hall, Derbyshire, and was completed by 1803. The Court of Directors of the East India Company found the high cost of all this magnificence not at all to their taste.

European Justice at Work: watercolour depicting the murder trial of a young Brahmin who killed his wife with a fish-knife because of her affair with the *mahant* (chief priest) of a nearby temple. This celebrated murder took place in Calcutta in 1873.

Lieutenant-Colonel W. R. Gilbert and other British officers being entertained with a *nautch* by the Raja of Sambalpur (Orissa). This is one of a set of twelve drawings made by an Indian artist for Gilbert (1785-1853); he shared his brother-in-law Charles D'Oyly's intense interest in art and formed a collection of Indian paintings.

Scroll painting, *c.* 1830, of the Raja of Tanjore in procession, followed by a European on horseback, probably the British Resident.

Drawing by a native artist, *c.* 1805, of Indian gerbils. This drawing from the Wellesley Collection is one of 2666 depicting animals, plants, birds, insects and fishes. Wellesley's keen interest encouraged the growth of research into natural history. In 1804 he issued a Minute on Natural History: 'many of the most common quadrupeds and birds of this country are either altogether unknown to the naturalist, or have been imperfectly and inaccurately described. The illustration and improvement of that important branch of natural history . . . is worthy of the munificence and liberality of the East India Company, and must necessarily prove an acceptable service to the world.'

View of Lucknow in 1860. The capital and seat of the Nawabs of Oudh, Lucknow was annexed by the British in 1856. When the Mutiny broke out in the following year, it became a major centre of insurgence. The Residency, in which was sheltering the entire European community, was besieged for three months until it was relieved on 25 September by a small force under Sir Henry Havelock. The final relief under Sir Colin Campbell did not come until 17 November. The Lucknow cemetery contains the graves of 2000 men, women and children.

The Young Ladies' Toilet, an illustration from *Sketches Illustrating the Manners and Customs of the Indians and Anglo-Indians* (1842) by William Tayler, who served in the Bengal Civil Service.

Watercolour self-portrait of Captain John Johnson sketching a waterfall in the Purwar river (Mysore). Johnson (*c.* 1769-1846) served with the Bombay engineers from 1785 until 1816, much of his career being spent in survey work. He returned to England via Persia, Georgia and Russia and in 1818 published *A Journey from India to England*. Like many British engineers in India, he was a skilled amateur artist: they have left a unique record of the Indian countryside and its antiquities.

Ootacamund in the Nilgiri Hills, Madras, a painting by Captain Richard Barron, 1835, 'taken from the bridge looking at the South side of the Lake. The distant hill is Dodabet, 8760 ft., the highest of the Nilgiris.'

grasses and ferns, and the foot of the cliffs, just where the waves plash, is covered with a thick velvety carpet of vivid emerald moss. Then you pass the mouth of a long, narrow valley running up and up until it ends in grey, misty distance. Here and there on a hilltop in a clearing a small cluster of Mugh huts built on piles, and sturdy Mugh women in scarlet petticoats and blue jackets crawling up the steep hillside with water jars on their heads.

All Beames' descriptions bring life in India very close; here is an evocation of the Chittagong monsoon in a letter to a friend written in August 1878:

You up-country fellows never see rain like we have here. It begins early in the morning before daybreak on the first of the month, and when you go to bed at ten o'clock on the 31st it is still drizzling on in the same remorseless way. Your boots grow a crop of mould every night. My beloved books, the only things that keep me going, are losing their bindings, and curling up into limp masses of pulp. The green mould crops out all over the damp, unwholesome walls, rank weeds grow all up the hillsides, and the rain carves out great gutters ending in a 'moraine' of muddy, fetid slush at the bottom. Whatsoever things are loathsome, whatsoever things are slimy, whatsoever things are stinking, sickening, ghastly, oozy, decaying and decayed, morbiferous, faeculent, miasmatic, malarious, and repulsive – these things abound. And over everything steadily, slowly, pitilessly, drenchingly, comes down by night and by day the dull, deadly rain like a pall covering the flaccid corpse of the soil.

Post Runner, a painting by Rapur Singh, 1866.

Eighteenth-century sketch of a European soldier carried by four bearers in a *palanquin*.

This is not an attempt at fine writing though it looks like it – I am too low in spirits for that! It is only an effort to put on paper the impression made on me as I sit in my veranda looking out at the sodden landscape below me.

Beames' descriptions of his work and the administrative machine are particularly valuable. Here he is on the role of the magistrate-collector, that job which Munro fought so hard to keep united:

The Magistrate-Collector of an Indian district is supposed to be very much what Joseph was in the Egyptian prison, 'whatsoever was done therein, he was the doer thereof'. From vaccination to education; from warding off a famine to counting the blankets of convicts in his jail; from taking a census to feeding an army on the march, all falls on him. If he protests in the least, or fails to do everything satisfactorily, he is punished by stoppage of promotion, public censure and removal to a less important post; if he does everything well, he may, perhaps . . . get some reward.

At one of the stations in Bengal, Purneah, he was faced with a problem all district officers encountered many times in their career: sanitation. Europe was learning fast the benefits of good sanitation; India's overwhelming sanitary

problems were attacked with zeal, though not always with lasting success. Beames' description of Purneah show us the extent of the problem:

Purneah, though called a town, was in reality a collection of small, scattered hamlets dropped down promiscuously in a swamp and buried in a luxurious overgrowth. Everywhere one came upon pools of black, stagnant water covered with weeds and fetid from receiving the sewage of the adjacent houses. Dark slimy patches of mud haunted by myriads of vermin bordered the narrow, winding roads; the walls of houses and huts were green with mould, every hedge and thicket was used as a latrine, and the smells were indescribable. . . . We did what we could by setting up a staff of sweepers to remove refuse and filth, cutting down the jungle, and fining people for not keeping their premises clean. Drains were made and kept clean, roads and bridges mended and a few other improvements were introduced. It got to be a regular habit with me to ride around the town every morning, attended by the Overseer, giving orders and seeing they were carried out. But it was a hopeless task, and I was not very successful. Malarious fever was permanently endemic, . . . cholera was seldom entirely absent, and the whole population was anaemic, stunted and cachetic.

John Beames' home life was typical too of the Victorian civilian. His fiancée, Ellen, came out to join him, and they married in December 1859 in a friend's drawing-room in Delhi and then went straight to Beames' first station in the Punjab. 'I could write much about the perfect happiness of my married life and my dear wife's excellencies, but such things are too sacred to be written about.' As a result, we get no idea at all of Ellen as a person; but Beames does inadvertently tell us a great deal about a woman's life in India then. The local Punjabis found Ellen a puzzle:

> So my wife was a startling novelty and the women in the remoter villages would crowd round the camp peering shyly at her, and there were, I was told, hot discussions as to whether she was a man or a woman. The absence of a beard was advanced in favour of the latter view, while the fact of her riding on horseback seemed a strong argument for the former.

Riding twenty miles brought on her first miscarriage. Beames says sternly:

Travelling in the Night Dak, a pencil drawing by Captain Robert Smith from his beautifully handwritten book *Pictorial Journal of Travels in Hindustan, from 1828 to 1833*.

Englishman riding in a dogcart, *c.* 1860. John Beames wrote of Calcutta in about 1858 that: 'About 12 we usually went out either in a buggy or a palki, custom having appointed this, the hottest time of the day, for making calls. Buggies are seldom seen in Calcutta now, the present generation preferring dogcarts. But a buggy has a hood which a dogcart has not, and it is therefore more suited for going out in the middle of the day.'

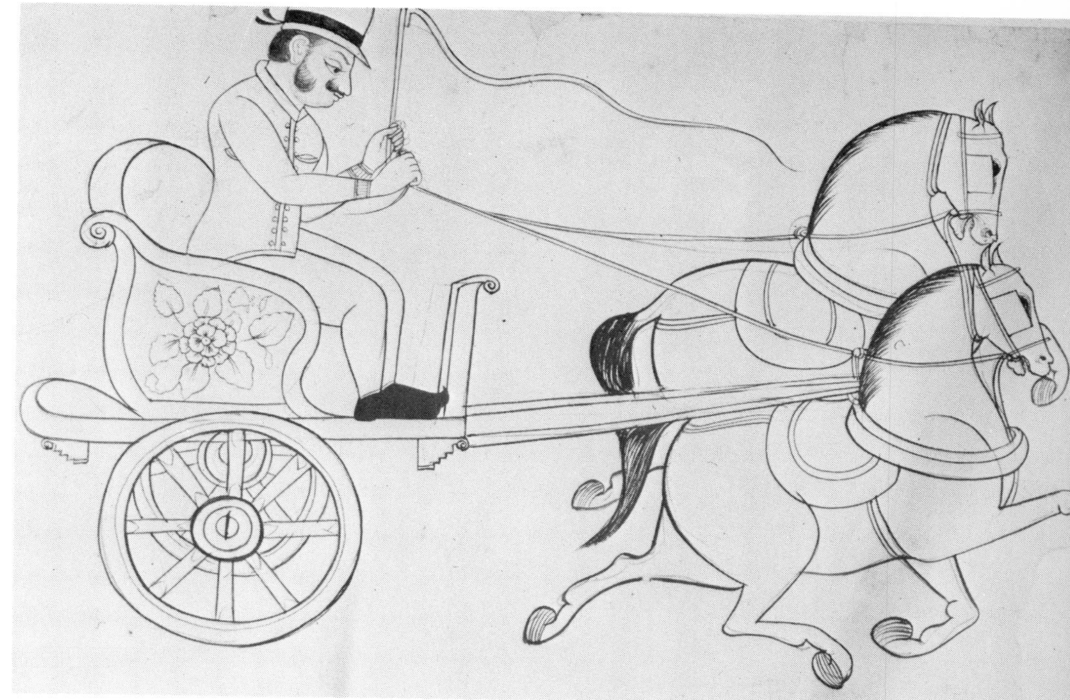

The ignorance of matters relating to their health when married, in which many young Englishwomen are brought up, often leads in India, where they have no older woman to advise them, to disastrous consequences. My wife did not know in her condition she ought not to ride, and a long and tedious illness was the consequence.

The nearest European doctor was thirty miles away. It is not surprising that many Englishwomen, and their babies, died in childbirth. Ellen Beames was to have eight children and further miscarriages before her days in India were over; she must have had a tough constitution. The frequent confinements of Victorian women go some way towards explaining how little part they played in founding and maintaining the Raj. With few exceptions – Annette Ackroyd in the field of education being one of them – women have no important place in the history of the British in India. They had an effect on social life: as more and more of them came out, Englishmen got married and established settled homes and therefore mixed less with wider Indian society. But it is wrong to blame, as many have, the arrival of women for the narrowing of outlook that took place during the Victorian era. Francis Hutchins, in his study of British imperialism, wrote that:

Englishwomen did not personally cause a narrowing of outlook in English society and a widening of the gap between the two races. . . . It seems more correct to say that British Indian society caused a narrowing of outlook among Englishwomen by refusing them the opportunity of pursuing interests outside its confining limits.

'Woman' was pure, delicate, unsuited to active life, the weaker sex in every way; 'man' was dominant, vigorous, hard-working and hard-playing, and no Victorian in India busy trying to belong to a 'middle-class aristocracy' would dream of disturbing these heartening generalizations. It was simply 'not done'

Watercolour by J. B. Bellasis entitled *Our 'Turnout', Bombay*. Major Bellasis is riding in a *tikka-gharri* with his wife and daughter Louie.

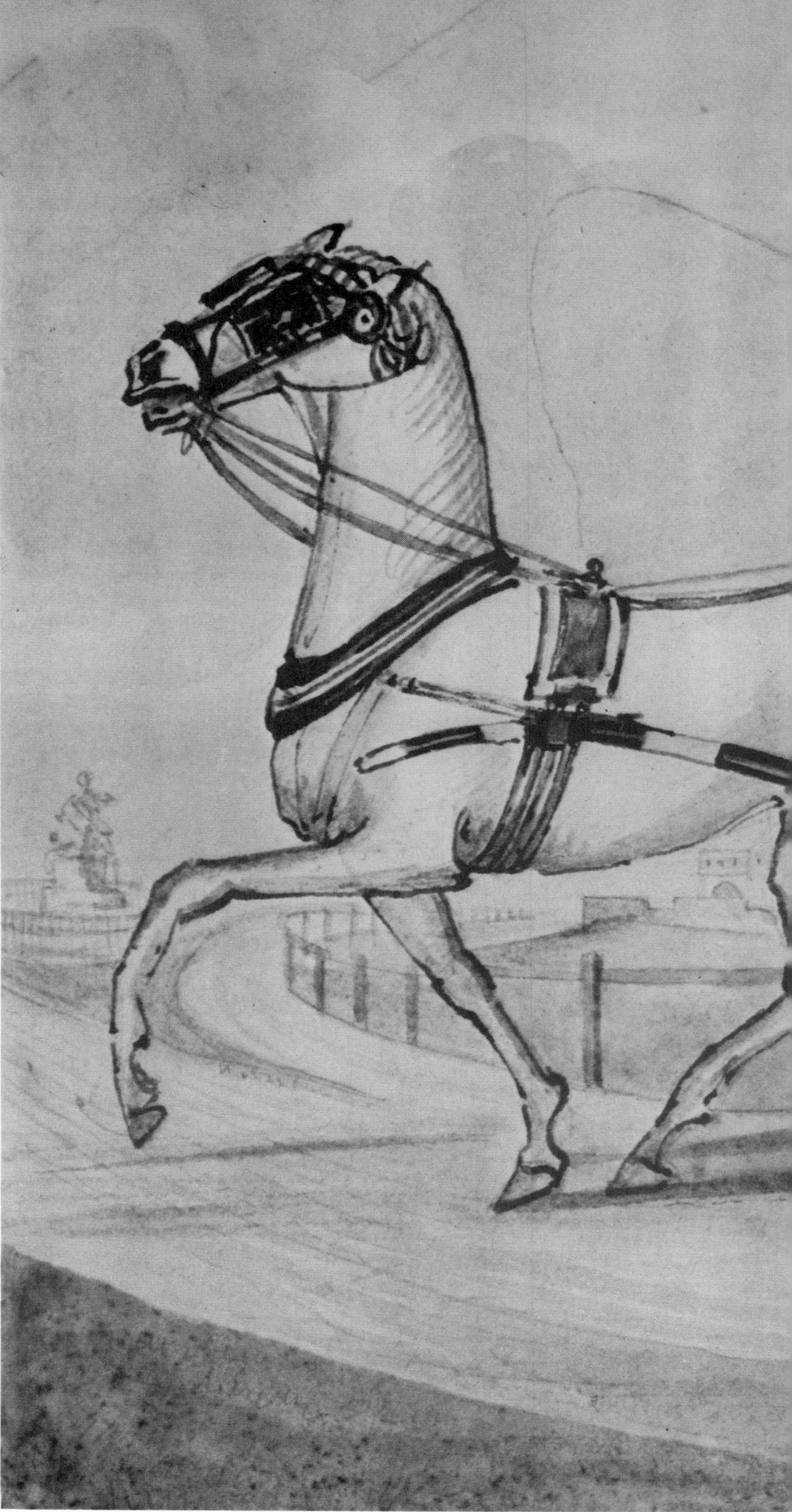

The Doctor's Wife out for a Drive, one of a series of illustrations about 'Life On Our Station'. The wife of the miserly doctor, McGhee, rides in a trap pulled by a camel, a beast which eats less than a horse. (Camels are only found in the north of India.) The elegant horse-drawn equipage behind only serves to point up the contrast.

Woodcut of a Sikh railway train. A European lady sits in the front carriage (though it is the third carriage of the train if it is put together); in the fifth carriage is a European Sahib. Notice that Indian men and women are segregated.

The loop – known as 'Agony Point' – on the Darjeeling railway. Sand had to be spread in front of the wheels to make them bite on the steep gradients.

for Englishwomen to break free of the restrictions that society had created for them; social ostracism would result, and social ostracism on a small station where five or six English families depended on each other for company and comfort was unthinkable. Luckily for Englishwomen, the First World War demolished the restrictions.

John Beames could be thought of as that 'strange abstraction, the average district officer'; he and his wife typify the Victorian couple spending an ordinary Indian Civil Service career in India: hard work, splendid moments, separation for years on end as children were taken back to England and looked after there. In fact, many men preferred to be on their own in India: to them India was man's work, best done unencumbered. They loved their work and lived only for it. Here is G. O. Trevelyan describing with rosy enthusiasm what a civilian in India was like in the 1860s:

> I know of no better company in the world than a rising young civilian. There is an entire absence of the carping pining spirit of discontent which is so painfully apparent in able men at home who . . . want interest or money. . . . It is impossible for the civilian to have any misgiving concerning the dignity and importance of his work. His power for good and evil is almost unlimited. . . . He is the member of an official aristocracy owning no social superior; bound to no man; fearing no man. . . . He is well aware that his advancement does not hang upon the will and pleasure of this or that other great man but is regulated by the opinions entertained of his ability and character by the service in general. . . . A civilian . . . makes it his aim to turn off his work in good style, trusting for his reward to the sense and public spirit of his

Sealdah railway station towards the end of the nineteenth century.

The Indus bridge under construction in the late nineteenth century.

chief. . . . He never speaks of his duties save in a spirit of enthusiasm or of his profession without a tone of profound satisfaction. . . .

But, besides the blessings of absorbing work, a civilian enjoys the inestimable comfort of freedom from pecuniary troubles. . . . Tom's assistant-magistrate keeps four horses and lives well within as many hundred rupees a month. If a man puts off his marriage to within a year or two of the age at which he may take a wife in England without being disinherited, he may always have a good house and plenty of servants, his champagne and his refrigerator, his carriage and buggy, an Arab for the Mem Sahib and for himself a hundred guinea horse that will face a pig without flinching. He will be able to portion his daughters and send his son to Harrow and Oxford; he may retire to a villa at Esher or a farm in his native county with a pension of a thousand a year and as much more from the interests of his savings.

Trevelyan sums up the progress of British society in India through the eyes of a typical Victorian:

It has generally been found that a manly valiant race which has imposed its yoke upon an effeminate and unwarlike people, in course of time, degenerates and becomes slothful and luxurious. . . . With the English in the East precisely the opposite result has taken place. The earliest settlers were indolent, dissipated, grasping, almost Orientals in their way of life, and almost heathens in the matter of religion. But each generation of their successors is more simple, more hardy, more Christian than the last.

The mores of an easier, more relaxed period of social behaviour, open to Indian influences and habits, get short shrift from the stern and proper Victorians.

An empire is built not only on sound government and efficient civil and legal administration but also on good communications. India had lamentably bad and few roads, and as the nineteenth century progressed British administrators attacked the problem energetically. In 1839 the Company's engineers embarked on building the Grand Trunk Road from Calcutta to Delhi, over a thousand miles; this road was described lyrically by a contemporary as being 'smooth as a bowling green' and was immediately full of traffic – bullock cart, camel and buffalo. More trunk roads followed quickly. But one still travelled along these improved roads by way of very slow methods, posting by *palanquin* being the most common. The European occupant reclined at full length in these 'little carriages without wheels'. Four or more bearers carried the *palanquin* or *palkee*, with extra bearers to carry luggage. The East India Company organized the system. If, in say 1845, as James Douglas recalled in his book on western India,

> you intended proceeding from Bombay to Calcutta you had to put yourself in communication with the head of the Postal Department, . . . giving him your destination etc. . . . As there are close upon a hundred halting stations, you will require to state how long you intend halting at each of them. . . . Bear in mind that your journey is one of 500 hours' duration. If it is April or May you will journey mostly by night and rest during the day. The reason why the Postmaster requires all these particulars is that the laying down a *dak* [post] to Calcutta involves an immense correspondence, and the route covers nearly 1,400 miles. . . . If your period is the rains, be thankful if you escape malaria, or if it is the hot weather, sunstroke.

Though this sounds very uncomfortable, one woman wrote cheerfully in 1838:

Palanquin travelling pleases me very much: I can sleep a good part of the night, and being able to sit up or lie down at pleasure, with plenty of room, I find it far less fatiguing than being cramped up all day in a carriage.

The coming of railways revolutionized India and opened it up not only for the British but for the Indians themselves. It is interesting that they should have developed so fast and so early in a country as backward both industrially and technically as India then was. India's first railways were financed by British capital (not by the Company); her first train ran from Bombay in November 1852. Here is a contemporary description by Lady Falkland of

Crossing Bamboo Bridge, 1894.

Gorai Bridge on the East Bengal railway seen from the north-west, c. 1869-72.

the first railroad opened in India. It can well be imagined what astonishment and excitement it caused among the natives, as well as what surprise it occasioned to many Europeans, for there were Anglo-Indians at Bombay, who had not been in Europe for many years, and who, therefore, had not seen a railroad.

A very handsome temple had been commenced before the railroad was contemplated, and was on the verge of completion when the latter was opened. A railway station, and a Hindoo temple in juxtaposition – the work of the rulers and the ruled.

The native Indian reaction to the railway was immediate: 'the railway took the fancy of the people at once, and the use of it became a national pastime, which continues in unbated vigour though the novelty has worn off,' said a civilian in the 1860s.

Even the ever-cautious Directors of the East India Company gradually became convinced of the soundness of the railways, particularly when they were told in 1853 that:

Bridge washed away by flood at Rampur Hat, Bengal, *c.* 1905.

A system of railways, judiciously selected and formed, would surely and rapidly give rise within this empire to the same encouragement of enterprise, the same multiplication of produce, the same discovery of latent resource, to the same increase of natural wealth, and to some similar progress in social improvement, that have marked the introduction of improved and extended communication in various kingdoms of the western world.

By 1880, about 2700 miles of railway had been built by the state and just over 6000 miles by private enterprise. By 1909, the figure was 31,500 miles in all, and most villages were within practical distance of a railway.

The impact on India of advanced communications was enormous; besides the obvious industrial and administrative advantages, the habit of rail travel helped to unify a vastly diverse people and to lessen the social barriers of caste and community; as a result political unification became more possible. The evils of famine were mitigated, and the economic isolation of villages broken down. Thoughtful romantics like Elphinstone would no doubt have lamented the passing of the ancient village economy and deplored the social evils industrialization brings. There is always a price to be paid for 'progress'.

The British also built canals, wells, hospitals, whole new townships.

> '*Why is my district death-rate low?*'
> *Said Binks of Hezabad,*
> '*Wells, drains and sewage-outfalls are*
> *My own peculiar fad.*'

Brigadier-General John Jacob (1812-58). After training at the East India Company's Addiscombe College, Jacob went to India in 1828 as a second lieutenant. His military action in Sind at the head of his own squadrons of irregular horse achieved both success and fame. But he always regarded military art as a means of bringing about civilization and peace. He gave his whole life for thirty years to the service of India and after he died his entire Sind squadrons and about 10,000 of the population of Jacobabad were present at the funeral.

Many energetic Englishmen made it their aim to improve the physical conditions of India: John Jacob, a fiery and singleminded man, achieved an amazing amount in the Baluchistan/Sind area above Karachi. He cleared and laid out 2589 miles of road, on which were 786 masonry bridges over navigable

canals also constructed by him. The simplest means were used to build these: a fire would be lit on a still day at the point to be reached, and the road or canal would be aimed directly at the smoke.

Jacob was a most unusual man; he had started off as a gunner, then became a cavalry leader, engineer and administrator, all of which he did superlatively well. He was obsessive; he never took leave and spent his private money and his pay on his improvements. He scorned fans, *punkahs* and ice and endured the heat without complaint, expecting all others to be as tough as he was. (It is not surprising he died youngish of 'brain fever'.) He founded a township called Jacobabad, which grew in seven years from a few huts to a town of seven thousand inhabitants, with a laboratory, engineers' and carpenters' workshops and a large library. A contemporary describes it in 1855:

> I have just returned from that wonderful place Jacobabad. Yesterday morning I went with Jacob nine miles into what four years ago was real desert . . . without a tree, a drop of water, or a blade of grass. . . . Now from the top of a surveying tower, as far as the eye could reach we could see the fields extended, the cultivators and cattle.

Another Englishman, Alfred Lyall, gave his name to a district called Lyallpur. Once a desert between rivers in the Punjab, this was a huge planned area to be made fertile by irrigation; a whole new countryside was designed – roads, railways, railway stations, market towns, villages; the mosque, temple, and school; magistrates' court, police station, groves of trees for shade; nothing was forgotten. This idea of Utopia not only came into being but actually worked. It is still working: by 1941 this district had a population of one and a quarter million and a cultivated area of one and a half million acres. It has been said by Philip Woodruff that 'if the English were to choose one monument by which their years in India were to be remembered, it might well be the canals, the cotton, and the prosperous villages of Lyallpur.'

4 The Pen and the Sword

Take up the White Man's Burden –
Send forth the best ye breed –
Go bind your sons in exile
To serve your captives' need;
To wait in heavy harness
On fluttered folk and wild –
Your new-caught, sullen peoples,
Half devil and half child . . .

wrote Rudyard Kipling in a famous poem; notice the words he uses to describe the 'Burden': the Englishman is bound in exile, serving in heavy harness. Equally loaded are his words for the Indians themselves: new-caught, sullen peoples who, as well as being aimless and wild, are also a mixture of devil and child. Famous this poem may be, but it gives a wildly distorted picture of the Raj. Think of all those eager, happy, hard-working Englishmen, and 'heavy harness' is quite wrong; remember the respect and affection for the Indian and the understanding of his way of life possessed by many enlightened men who served in India from the early days, and a phrase like 'half devil and half child' becomes a sweeping condemnation which is not only offensive but also not representative of the British view.

For there is no doubt that the British cared about India and the Indians. As dominion grew during the eighteenth century, so did the sense of responsibility, as we have seen. Care for India's physical and social well-being continued apace: ambitious programmes of irrigation, of the building of roads, canals, bridges, railways, new townships were carried out. Nor did the British neglect India's administrative, legal and civil problems. This book has described the growth of the Company's civil arm, a unique aspect of any trading company; but as for India's spiritual and mental well-being, here was thorny ground on which the East India Company had no desire whatever to tread.

Company policy was deliberate: no interference in native religions and ways of living. The Indians had their own complex religions and even more complex caste system; the Company did not wish to disturb these by imposing Christianity and its manners and mores on the inhabitants. This respect stemmed partly from enlightened motives but mainly from indifference and commercial expediency.

The Company sent out chaplains for the spiritual welfare of their own British employees, but they were forbidden to indulge in mission outside the British population. (The sort of clergymen who mostly went out preferred business to mission anyway.) Risky people like missionaries, who were educational and social reformers as well, were not allowed by the Company to go to India. As J. W. Kaye, the eminent nineteenth-century historian of India, put it:

> India was a close preserve in the hands of the East India Company. To go there without a licence from the Company was to become a poacher, and to incur the risk of being sent ignominiously home. A man without a covenant was in the Company's estimation a dangerous person; doubly dangerous such a one with a Bible.

Reform of any sort was bad for business. Alas for the Company; the age of reform was upon them, whether they wanted it or not.

Our Padre, who is here seen lighting his cigar as he leaves a grieving couple and rushes on his way. His brisk though annually repeated sermons and speedy services go down well: 'the sick in hospital are visited and attended zealously and lovingly, though he does drive a dog-cart, patronise the races, and burn the midnight oil over a pool at billiards or at a rubber of whist.'

William Wilberforce (1759-1833), an unfinished portrait by Thomas Lawrence, 1828. Wilberforce took up politics as soon as he left Cambridge and remained a politician throughout his life. His transparent kindliness and simplicity made him loved even by his antagonists. Though an energetic philanthropist, he was never a fanatic about any of his causes.

Attitudes in England at the beginning of the nineteenth century were changing fast, and evangelicals with a burning zeal for reform were now influential men in Parliament. William Wilberforce is the best known; he was part of a group known as the Clapham Sect (because they all lived near each other in Clapham in south London) whose main aims were to abolish the Slave Trade and to open up India to missionary enterprise. Since two founder members of the sect, Sir Charles Grant and Sir John Shore, had served as civil servants in Bengal, their connections with India were strong and had a powerful effect on Company policy. In 1813, under great Parliamentary pressure, the Company granted permission for missionaries to work in India.

William Carey (1761-1834) with his chief *pundit*, Mritunjaya, after a painting by Robert Hume, *c.* 1812.

The Mission Church, Serampore, *c.* 1800. The first Bengali convert to Christianity was baptised in the river Hooghly just in front of the church. This church, and the nearby Serampore College, were both handsome buildings. Carey believed that: 'Beauty is an educative force, and that the mere presence of grandeur elevates the growing intellect; that an institution, housed anywhere, dies; whereas, enshrined in an adequate building, it will live through generations.'

Missionaries concentrated on education and on the translation and printing of the Bible into as many native tongues as possible. Often the language had not been properly written down before, so the missionaries prepared the first grammars and dictionaries. They also educated Indians, hoping to convert them: what happened instead was a flowering of Indian nationalism and of vernacular literature. Relatively few Indians became converted to Christianity despite Victorian evangelical optimism; but there is no doubt at all of the value of missionary achievement in education and in social reform, particularly of the lives of Indian women. These achievements underpinned the Raj that was to come; without them the Company's government would have remained on a superficial plane and would not have touched the heart of India at all. The full responsibility for the government of an empire would not have been taken up, and as a result the preparation for the final handing over of power would not have been so profoundly effective. The inter-reaction of government and missionary is neatly summed up by Kenneth Ingham in his book on *Reformers in India*:

Separated by more than a century from the magnificent urgency of the missionaries and the official conservatism of the East India Company's representatives, one can note the not infrequent recklessness of the former group and the feebleness so often displayed by the latter in their true perspective, as the normal offshoots of the combination of enthusiasm and steadiness which makes for lasting and valuable progress.

Although the East India Company only gave its official permission in 1813, some missionaries had already gone to India illegally. The most famous of these was William Carey, the first English missionary in India, who arrived in 1793, sent by the Baptist Mission Society. He and his family had a very rough time during their first few years; life was precarious without a licence, and the death of their eldest son and his wife's growing insanity added to Carey's worries. Fortunately he and two fellow-missionaries, William Ward and Joshua Marshman, were given security by the Danish at their settlement near Calcutta called Serampore. Here they founded a mission which became famous as a model of humane achievement. W. H. Russell, *The Times* correspondent sent out in 1858 to cover the Indian Mutiny, was taken within the first few days of his arrival in Calcutta to Serampore. In his *Indian Mutiny Diary* he writes:

> Crossed the river by boat near the railway station, where a carriage awaited us, and thence drove through thick woods of cocoa-plantains etc., lined with native huts and miserable villages – the Southwark of Calcutta – for some sixteen miles to the village or station of Serampore. . . . [It] is famous in the annals of missionary enterprise, and, let me add, of missionary devotion, if not success, in India, and the records of the good men's lives who made it the scene of their labours possess an enduring interest.

Carey, Ward and Marshman set up a printing press and worked indefatigably at translating the Bible and other works into various Indian languages. Carey, having thoroughly mastered Bengali, Hindi, Marathi, Persian, Punjabi, Telugu and, most important of all, Sanskrit, found the back of his task broken when these seven languages were learnt: secondary dialects could be quickly mastered. He personally translated the whole Bible into six languages, including Sanskrit and Assamese; he also translated various parts of the Bible into twenty-eight other languages. His friends Marshman and Ward were equally energetic and added Bibles in Chinese and Burmese. The group did not only concentrate on the Bible; they encouraged their *pundits* (Brahmins versed in Sanskrit) to write original works in their vernaculars and published these, thus founding modern Bengali literature. Dictionaries and grammars were compiled; a four-volume survey of Hindu history, literature and religion was also published. The industry of Carey, Marshman and Ward was great by any standards, and so was their linguistic ability.

Besides all their literary and missionary work, they found time for teaching; Carey himself was invited by Lord Wellesley to become one of the first teachers at Fort William College; and, after Haileybury was founded in England, Fort William continued as a small college for civilians posted to Bengal. Carey taught Sanskrit, Bengali and Marathi there and his open, unstuffy attitude made him a strong influence on young civilians in his care.

But the schools established by the missionaries themselves were their most important contribution to education. They were ideal pioneers in the field, because they knew that the spread of learning was an urgent matter and believed that they had to provide, to the best of their ability, teaching immediately at all levels, for anyone who was interested.

Until then, Indian education had been the prerogative and monopoly of the highest Hindu caste, the Brahmins. Only they were permitted to read the great Sanskrit scriptures. The Serampore missionaries broke this monopoly and gave Indians of all castes basic instruction. They then decided to found a college at Serampore to give Indians of however humble caste the opportunity of higher education; and their first concern was to offer the students access to their own Indian scriptures and classics, which had been locked away from them in Sanskrit. Carey gave Indian literature to ordinary Indians, with incalculable results.

Serampore College was opened in 1818. The two hundred students included low- and high-caste Indians, Hindu and Muslims; the majority of students were non-Christian. Carey felt it imperative that there should be no religious bias; students should come to learn the sciences, arts and theology for the joy of learning, and not for the hidden purpose of conversion to Christianity. He wrote:

> It will be time enough a hundred years hence, when the country is filled with knowledge, and truth has triumphed over error, to think of sects and parties. Every public institution, aiming at India's betterment, ought to be constructed on so broad a basis as to invite the aid of all denominations.

Carey believed that once Indians were instructed in their own philosophy, literature, religion and science, and also in Western literature, religion and science, they would be qualified to compare the two and choose for themselves. He had no doubt that in the end Indians would see the superiority of the Christian faith; knowledge first, followed by enlightenment. The result of his college was indeed knowledge and enlightenment, but not mass conversion to Christianity.

Carey was an extraordinarily gifted man; his humble background (he had been a shoemaker before he left England) did not hinder him in the least. As well as all his work of teaching and translation, he was a keen and very knowledgeable botanist and natural historian and believed that:

> A man must be in the habit of constantly examining fields, woods, and receptacles of water. . . . I have always had a strong turn for natural history, and especially for botany, and known nothing fitter to relax the mind after close application.

Carey founded his own botanical garden at Serampore and filled it with a vast number of Eastern plants. Here are his typically detailed instructions to his son Jabez who went as a missionary to Indonesia:

> Be sure to send me every possible vegetable production. . . . I shall be glad of the smallest as well as the largest common plants. Think none insignificant. Plant the small in boxes, and always keep some well-rooted and ready; if too recently planted, they die on the way. Just before despatching them, sow very thickly amongst them

The menagerie at Barrackpore, near Calcutta, 1848. As a result of the Marquess of Wellesley's interest, an 'Institution Promoting the Natural History of India', including a menagerie and an aviary, was established in the grounds of the Governor-General's house at Barrackpore.

seeds of trees, fruits and shrubs, covered with a finger's thickness of fresh soil. . . . Do send abundant seeds of every sort, perfectly ripe and dry, in named paper packets, in a box or basket, secured from the rats; and, if possible, cite the due soil. Parasitical plants, such as you have often seen me tie on trees, need only be stripped where they grow, and hung in baskets in any airy part of the ship, or even at the maintop. All boxes of plants must have strips of wood over them, to keep out the rats.

In charge of Calcutta's Botanical Gardens at that time was a great botanist, Dr William Roxburgh; Carey edited and printed at Serampore his friend Roxburgh's famous book *Flora Indica*. Lord Wellesley, no doubt influenced by these two men, founded an establishment 'Promoting the Natural History of India', which included a menagerie and an aviary, in the grounds of the

Sir Charles Edward Trevelyan (1807-86), Governor of Madras March 1859 to June 1860 and Financial Member of the Supreme Council 1863 to 1865.

Thomas Babington Macaulay, Lord Macaulay (1800-59), a portrait by F. Grant, 1863. Macaulay's early intellectual precosity and phenomenal memory were famous (he knew *Pilgrim's Progress* and the whole of *Paradise Lost* by heart). He was an industrious author and politician. Offered a seat on the Supreme Council of India, he went there in 1834; in three and a half years he achieved a vast amount.

Governor-General's house at Barrackpore (just across the river Hooghly from Serampore). He commissioned local artists to produce a fine series of descriptive pictures; one of the finest (and most delightful) is reproduced in the coloured illustrations after page 80. Lord Wellesley is best known for his grandiloquent gestures and his aristocratic disdain, particularly of his employers, those 'cheesemongers of Leadenhall Street' as he called them. The fact that he was fascinated by the minutiae of natural history is less well known.

During these years, when some of the British were deepening their knowledge of India, her literature, languages, history, flora and fauna, and were working towards establishing a broader educational system, other Englishmen were expressing a new idea: that English should become the official language of India. This clearly threw quite a different light on the whole question of education. Carey's emphasis, as we have seen, was to open up knowledge through the vernacular; he had no wish to anglicize Indians. But although he and others like him did not purposely intend it, they speeded up the westernizing process despite themselves; missionary hospitals, dispensaries, orphanages and schools represented the West in its best form to the average Indian. And as far as language was concerned, Indians needed a *lingua franca* amongst their diversity of tongues. They had had to learn Persian under the Mughals for all official business and government matters; why not substitute English for Persian, now that the Mughal Empire was moribund and the British were in control?

Powerful voices began arguing for English to become the official language of government, court and trade and also the language in which all higher learning should be taught. Two men had a decisive influence on events: one was a civilian, Charles Edward Trevelyan, who became the brother-in-law of the other decisive voice, Thomas Babington Macaulay. Macaulay went out to India in 1834 to take up his duties as law member of the Council of the Governor-General, Lord Bentinck; he took with him his sister Hannah, who met and married Trevelyan there.

Trevelyan, after a brilliant two years at Haileybury College, had gone out to India in 1827 to a junior post in Delhi. He impressed everyone from the start as an outstanding member of the Civil Service. He knew his own abilities; he wrote to his brother that he would not 'float through life, but would conquer'. At the age of twenty-four he was given the influential post of deputy secretary in the Political Department in Calcutta. He was a formidable, enterprising young man, intellectually brilliant and an able pig-sticker as well. His particular concern was with the education of Indians, and he fought the older, more conservative civilians in Calcutta for a reform of the government's educational policies. He wrote a famous pamphlet, *Education in India* (published in 1838), which gives us an exact picture of the liberal attitude in India then and thereafter.

The existing connexion between two such distant countries as England and India, cannot, in the nature of things, be permanent: no effort of policy can prevent the natives from ultimately regaining their independence. But there are two ways of arriving at this point. One of these is through the medium of revolution; the other, through that of reform. In one, the forward movement is sudden and violent; in the other, it is gradual and peaceable. . . . The only means at our disposal for preventing the one and securing the other class of results is, to set the natives on a process of European improvement, to which they are already sufficiently inclined. They will then cease to desire and aim at independence on the old Indian footing. . . . The political education of a nation is a work of time; and while it is in progress, we shall be as safe as it will be possible for us to be. The natives will not rise against us, we shall stoop to raise them; there will be no reaction, because there will be no pressure; the national activity will be fully and harmlessly employed in acquiring and diffusing European knowledge, and in naturalizing European institutions. . . . The change will thus be peaceably and gradually effected; there will be no struggle, no mutual exasperation; the natives will have independence, after first learning how to make good use of it; and we shall exchange profitable subjects for still more profitable allies. . . . A precarious and temporary relation will almost imperceptibly pass into another far more durable and beneficial. Trained by us to happiness and independence, and endowed with our learning and political institutions, India will remain the proudest monument of British benevolence; and we shall long continue to reap, in the affectionate attachment of the people, and in a great commercial intercourse with their splendid country, the fruit of that liberal and enlightened policy which suggested to us this line of conduct.

When the Macaulays met this fiery, idealistic young man, they took to him at once; his views made sense to people brought up in the high moral atmosphere of the Clapham Sect. Here is part of Macaulay's letter home describing his brother-in-law's character:

Trevelyan is a most stirring reformer. . . . His principles I believe to be excellent and his temper very sweet. . . . He is rash and uncompromising in public matters. If he were a wrong-headed and narrow-minded man, he would be a perfect nuisance. But he has so strong an understanding that, though he often goes too fast, he scarcely ever goes in the wrong direction. . . .

His manners are odd, blunt almost to roughness at time, and at other times awkward even to sheepishness. But when you consider that . . . he was in a remote province of India, where his whole time was divided between Public business and field sports, and where he seldom saw a European gentleman and never a European lady, you will not wonder at this. There is nothing vulgar about him. . . . His face has a most characteristic expression of ardour and impetuosity. . . . His mind is full of schemes of moral and political improvement and his zeal boils over in all his talk. . . . He is by no means so good a wooer as a financier and diplomatist. . . . His lovemaking, though very ardent and sincere, is as awkward as you could wish to see. . . . His topics, even in courtship, are steam navigation, the education of natives.

Trevelyan's arguments about education were firmly supported by his new friend Macaulay, who wrote a famous Minute which persuaded the Governor-General to decide in favour of English as the official language. As Macaulay put it, his bias quite clear for all to see, the question was

whether the funds employed by Government for the purposes of education should be employed in teaching Arabic and Sanskrit, the medicine of Galen, the astronomy of Ptolemy and the fables of the Hindu mythologies, or in communicating European knowledge by means of the English language. There was not a single question which did not resolve itself into the one great question: English or Sanskrit, Newton or Ptolemy, the Vedas or Adam Smith, the Mahabharata or Milton, the sun round the

John Bull Converting the Indians, an illustration by Thomas Rowlandson from *Qui Hi* by Quiz, published in 1816. *Qui Hi* is a long satirical poem about life in India, of which various aspects were attacked; the East India Company was criticized for corruption and military oppression. A major point was British indifference to Hindu customs. In this picture, John Bull is shown as an absentee landlord who, after taking land revenue from the natives, threatens to foist the Bible on the three: Muslim, Parsee and Hindu Brahmin.

earth or the earth round the sun, the medicine of the Middle Ages or the medicine of the nineteenth century.

On 7 March 1835, English became the official language of India; all higher education was to be taught in English, which would also from now on be used instead of Persian in diplomacy, government business and the higher courts of law. The substitution of English for Persian was of far-reaching importance as far as the Raj was concerned. Middle-class Indians, some of whom would formerly have learnt Persian as a means of livelihood, now learnt English. The English language exposed them to a whole new world of Western influences. Into the Hindu consciousness entered moral and spiritual ideas strange to him, such as the worth of the individual, the equality of all before God, the primacy of conscience and reason. The freedom of the individual to think for himself was a challenge to the whole orthodox Hindu system of tradition and authority.

One can see why the Company diehards were against education in English: it gave the Indians intellectual weapons they would rather have kept exclusive to the rulers. As it was, the combination of English as the *lingua franca*, making accessible Western ideas, and the encouragement of the vernacular tradition by men like Carey, meant that a healthy balance was achieved. The British became less mysterious to the Indians, who absorbed what they needed of British ideas and culture and made a synthesis of their own. The vernaculars were not superseded by English; they are still spoken, and so is English. A congress of

Indian writers in 1971 stated that: 'The inescapable reality is that English continues to be the only expedient language throughout India.' The tension which is needed for a healthy balance is there, 150 years later. (But the early champions of education would be depressed by the fact that seven out of ten Indians in 1978 still cannot read or write.)

The new Victorians like Macaulay and Trevelyan found the careful opinions of the 'old hands' like Munro and Malcolm irritatingly out of date. Munro had written despairingly in 1821:

I have no faith in the modern doctrine of the rapid improvement of the Hindoos, or of any other people. The character of the Hindoos is probably much the same as when Vasco da Gama first visited India, and it is not likely that it will be much better a century hence.

When I read, as I sometimes do, of a measure by which a large province had been suddenly improved, or a race of semi-barbarians civilized almost to Quakerism, I throw away the book.

In his book *The Political History of India from 1784 to 1823*, John Malcolm wrote this analysis of the role of government:

We must divest our minds of all arrogant pretensions arising from the presumed superiority of our knowledge, and seek the accomplishment of the great ends we have in view by the means which are best suited to the peculiar nature of the objects. . . . That time may gradually affect a change, there is no doubt; but the period is as yet distant when that can be expected; and come when it will, to be safe or beneficial, it must be . . . the work of society itself. All that government can do is, by maintaining the internal peace of the country, and by adapting its principles to the various feelings, habits and character of its inhabitants, to give time for the slow and silent operation of the desired improvement, with a constant impression that every attempt to accelerate this end will be attended with the danger of its defeat.

His words sum up the balanced and enlightened views of the last exponents of the age of reason.

By 1835, Munro and Malcolm were dead; reform was the order of the day. Once English became the official language, 'progress' and 'improvement' were hurried on by legislation. The British were by now impatient of opinions like Malcolm's that 'great and beneficial alterations in policy, to be complete, must be produced within the society itself, they cannot be the mere fabrication of its superiors, or of a few who deem themselves enlightened.' Wise words; however the new men did deem themselves enlightened – in many respects they were – and they took no heed of caution. The future was bright; they had complete faith in their ideas and abilities.

William Wilberforce made a speech in Parliament in 1813 which illustrates his total evangelical confidence in the superiority of Great Britain:

Let us endeavour to strike our roots into the soil by the gradual introduction and establishment of our own principles and opinions; of our laws, institutions, and manners; above all, as the source of every other improvement, of our religion, and consequently of our morals. . . . Are we so little aware of the vast superiority even of European laws and institutions, and far more of British institutions, over those of Asia, as not to be prepared to predict with confidence, that the Indian community which should have exchanged its dark and bloody superstitions for the genial influence of civil order and security, of social pleasures and domestic comforts, as to be desirous of preserving the blessings it should have acquired; and can we doubt that it would be bound even by the ties of gratitude to those who have been the honoured instruments of communicating them?

His friend Charles Grant, also a member of the Clapham Sect and three times Chairman of the Court of Directors of the East India Company, decided categorically that the Hindus were 'a race of men lamentably degenerate and base', going on to say in his book, cumbersomely entitled *Observations on the State of Society among the Asiatic Subjects of Great Britain, particularly with respect to Morals*, that:

In considering the affairs of the world as under the control of the Supreme Disposer, and those distant territories . . . providentially put into our hands . . . is it not necessary to conclude that they were given to us, not merely that we might draw an annual profit from them, but that we might diffuse among their inhabitants, long sunk in darkness, vice, and misery, the light and benign influence of the truth, the blessings of well-regulated society, the improvements and comforts of active industry? In every progressive step of this work, we shall also serve the original design with which we visited India, that design still so important to this country – the extension of our commerce.

General Stringer Lawrence (1697-1775), a portrait by Thomas Gainsborough. Lawrence's military career in India was spent defending British trading interests against the rival French company, whose army was led by General Dupleix. Lawrence's successes included the defeat of the French at Bahur in August 1752 and the successful defence of Trichinopoly in 1754.

Profitable commerce in return for Western enlightenment: a useful balance in their eyes. Men as different as John Malcolm and William Carey would have disapproved of this kind of religio-commercial expediency; because their work was practical and at grass-roots level, their humane attitudes helped to keep the balance in India while the wordy theorists back in England were busily trying to upset it.

Positive dogmatic men like Trevelyan believed firmly in the concept of progress; he, with many other Haileybury-trained men, brought about often necessary reforms in land tenure and education with well-meaning rigidity which made many enemies amongst influential Indians. It was inevitable that all these brisk efficient Englishmen with their heads full of theories and hearts full of zeal would alienate the Indians: it is not surprising that, in time, some

Bheestie and *mehtar*. A *bheestie* was a native water-carrier; *mehtar* was a term used ironically when addressing a sweeper. Literally it meant 'prince'.

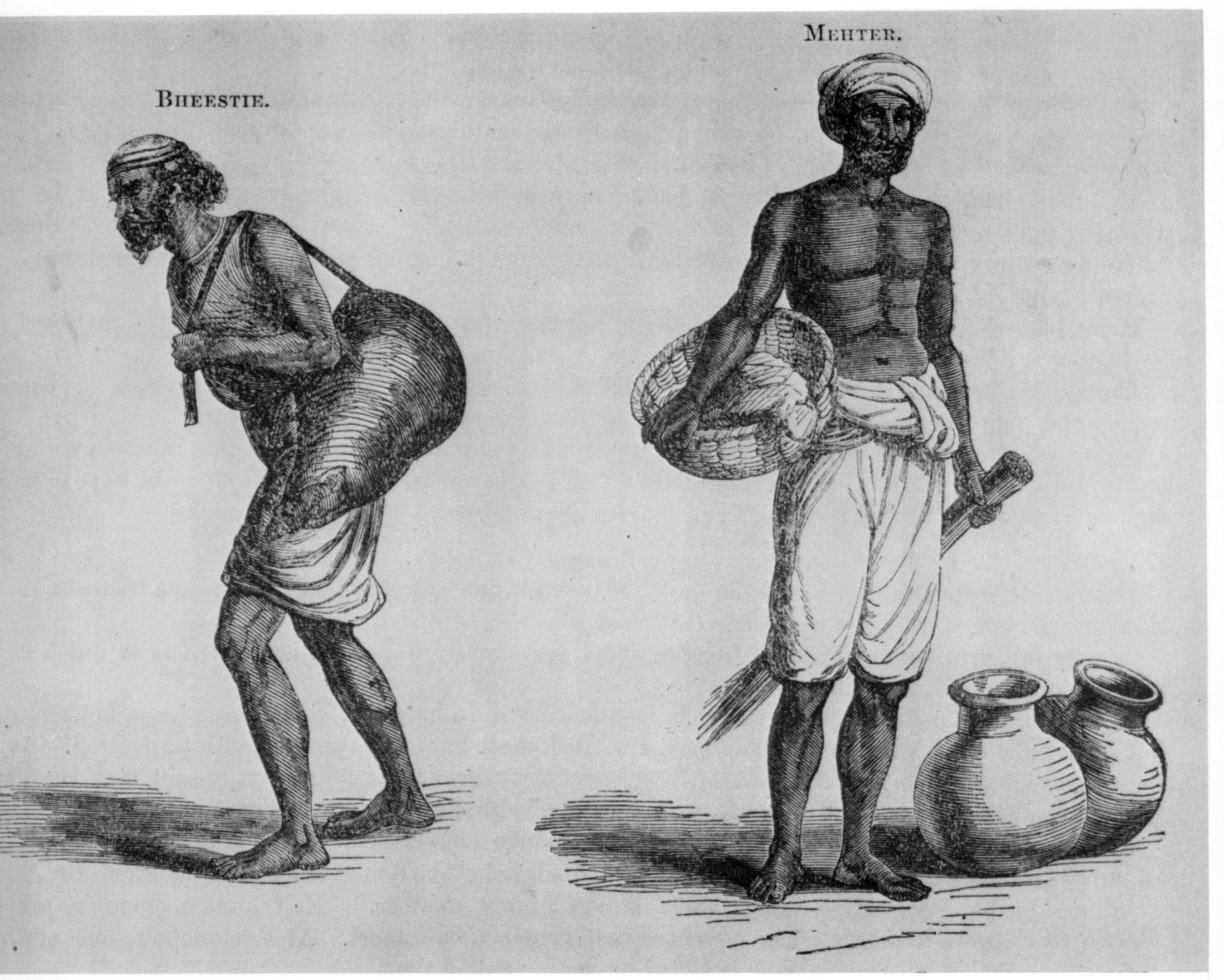

Sweepers (*domes*) of untouchable caste. They cleaned and emptied the latrines.

of them rebelled. The many causes of the Indian Mutiny of 1857 are too complex to be gone into here; but at the heart of them was a real fear of a religious and ideological take-over by the British. The fear was in some ways well founded: by the 1830s many of the top British in India belonged to the evangelical movement; they were a highly influential minority who believed that Divine Providence had sent them to India to convert it to Christianity and to Western ideas. The utter lack of understanding of the Indian that was prevalent amongst some civil servants makes distressing reading now. Lord Moira (Marquess of Hastings), who was Governor-General from 1813 to 1823, wrote in his Journal (later published) for the edification of his children back in England:

The Hindu appears a being nearly limited to mere animal functions, and even in them indifferent. Their proficiency and skill in the several lines of occupation to which they are restricted, are little more than the dexterity which any animal with similar conformation, but with no higher intellect than a dog, an elephant, or a monkey, might be supposed capable of attaining.

No wonder the ideas of these 'lowly animals' were considered gross, base and idolatrous. 'Brahminism is the most monstrous system of interference and oppression that the world has ever seen,' wrote J. W. Kaye. 'It could be maintained only by ignorance and superstition of the grossest kind.' Today one would feel, with Philip Mason, 'that even if Sanskrit geography and physics were wide of the mark, there was much wisdom in the philosophy and religion that accompanied them', an opinion that would doubtless be shared by men like Elphinstone, Malcolm and Carey.

But as the nineteenth century progressed, sympathy for and interest in Indian beliefs waned. Evangelical ideas spread through a large majority, both civilian and military, of the British in India. A colonel admitted in 1857 that 'as to the question whether I have endeavoured to convert sepoys [native soldiers, from the Persian *sipah*, an army] and others to Christianity, I would humbly reply that this has been my object.'

Pani-wallahs or water-carriers.

Painting by an Indian artist of a Hindu priest garlanding the flags of the 35th Bengal Light Infantry at the Presentation of the Colours ceremony, *c.* 1847.

It is therefore not surprising that, although the British government did not have a policy to convert India, Indians themselves began to fear that it was simply waiting for the right moment to introduce a mass conversion by law. To Indians everything seemed to point that way: missionary activity, the official use of English, the reorganization of land and property rights, the compulsory breaking of rules of caste in the Army. It was this last that set light to the fuse that led to the explosion of rebellion: soldiers had to bite off the ends of their cartridges before loading them (standard drill at the time), and sepoys learnt that in future cartridges were to be greased with tallow made from animal fat containing the fat of cows and pigs. Amongst Hindus, to eat beef is the deepest degradation; for Muslims, to eat pork. Thus the Mutiny began.

The caste system of India, that complex and mysterious thing, was always a puzzle to the British. It was in the Army that they came into close contact with caste; in civilian and commercial walks of life they could more or less ignore it and do no more than marvel at a religious rule that commanded a poor Hindu to throw away the food he was preparing as polluted should a passing European's shadow fall upon it. In the Army prohibitions of caste had to be considered all the time, and in the early days British officers were tolerant and often sympathetic. In return sepoys were willing to compromise a little, particularly when on campaign. But some did not; a Brahmin *subadar* (captain) dying of heat, thirst and loss of blood was offered water from a leather bottle by General Skinner but refused to drink. Brahmins are forbidden to drink water that has not been drawn by a man of the right grade; they are also forbidden to touch leather.

Brahmins were ritually the highest caste, but caste has nothing necessarily to do with class, as the British continually discovered. Brahmins were priests and scholars but could also be low class – cooks or messengers. The next highest caste, the Rajputs, were kings, barons, landowners, soldiers; the third caste, the Vaisyas, were traders, bankers and money-lenders. Sudras, the fourth caste, were artisans, cultivators, clerks, and those who did certain domestic tasks which did not pollute; they were *palanquin*-bearers for instance. The polluting jobs of sweepers, soil-carriers, scavengers, skinners etc. were all done by 'untouchables', who were outside the caste system. Each group including the untouchables had restrictions about whom they could marry or mix with; there were also complicated rules about preparing food, eating, drinking, smoking and washing. It was obvious that sepoys had to compromise their caste rules slightly; but the British allowed them latitude and, for example, permitted

Tom Raw Rejects the Embraces of the Nabob of Bengal: illustration from *Tom Raw, the Griffin*, a Burlesque poem in twelve cantos sub-titled 'The Adventures of a Cadet in the East India Company's Service', 1828. A 'griffin' was a man newly arrived in India; griffinage lasted for a year.

sepoys to prepare their own food, which made the Army as a whole less efficient but the individual sepoy happy and therefore a better soldier.

From the very early settlement days, sepoys had been hired by the Company to guard and defend its property. These early soldiers were a ragged, ill-disciplined lot, who looked, as a Governor of Bombay put it in 1704, 'more like bandits in the woods than military men'. It took the British 150 years to realize the valour and military usefulness of the sepoy and to incorporate him formally, in about 1750, into the framework of the three Presidency Armies, of Bombay, Madras and Bengal. The two men most responsible for the transformation of the 'rabble of peons' into an efficient infantry were Robert Clive and his Commander-in-Chief, General Stringer Lawrence. Stringer Lawrence, called the 'father of the Indian Army', was an outstanding personality. To look at him, with his large paunch and double chin, one would hardly have imagined him a fighting officer. In fact, he was a robust and energetic tactician, always ready to attack the French, who were trying hard to drive the British out of India. Lawrence was tetchy and bad-tempered, but his tantrums were the sort his followers related to each other with pride rather than with exasperation.

Lawrence also possessed the power to inspire the sepoys with confidence;

Scinde Camel Corps, a watercolour by J. B. Bellasis.

A barrackroom off duty, 1863. Notice the complex system of *punkahs* cooling these bored soldiers.

they would do anything for him, and he in turn cherished them. He also knew that an inspiring leader cannot last for ever, so he worked steadily towards a permanent framework for the sepoys. He organized them into companies; he gave them uniforms, sensible rules which allowed for the complexity of the caste system and, most important of all, a special oath, simple and impressive, which bound the sepoy to a visible symbol of military honour, the regimental colours. The sepoy stood two paces in front of the colours, and with a person of his caste beside him swore the oath to

> serve the Honourable Company faithfully and truly against all their enemies, while I continue to receive their pay and eat their salt. I do swear to obey all the orders I may receive from my Commanders and Officers, never to forsake my post, abandon my colours or turn my back on my enemies and that I will in all things behave myself like a good and faithful sepoy in perfect obedience at all times to the rules and customs of war.

The important point to remember is that the enemies against whom the sepoy was to fight were his own countrymen; his loyalty as a soldier had indeed to be absolute. It was fortunate for the British that being in the Army was an honourable vocation for an Indian: it was a matter of pride that a father should bring his sons and male relatives from his village into his regiment. But, even so, the fact remained that a sepoy was being paid by the Company to help to conquer his own country for the glory and benefit of an alien power. As Thomas Munro wrote perceptively in 1817: 'We are trying an experiment never yet tried in the world, maintaining a foreign dominion by means of a native army.' By this time, the power of the British in India depended to a great extent on the native army, and any general with imagination could see the permanent difficulty of retaining the sepoy's fidelity. Sepoys greatly outnumbered the British soldiers; no wonder that John Malcolm said, 'In an Empire like India, we are always in danger.'

It was Charles Metcalfe who summed up with his usual brilliance the delicate balance of the British position:

> Some say our Empire in India rests on opinion, others on main force. It in fact depends on both. We could not keep the country by opinion if we had not a considerable force and no force that we could pay would be sufficient if it were not aided by the opinion of our invincibility. Our force does not operate so much by its actual strength as by the impression which it produces and that impression is the opinion by which we hold India.

Good officers were essential if this 'good opinion' were to be kept; and often the officers who came out from England in increasing numbers were not good enough. One officer, Major H. Bevan, who served in the Madras Army from 1808 until 1839, wrote in his memoirs: 'A great error committed by young officers on first joining the Indian Army is to affect contempt for the soldiers whom they are to command calling them black fellows, niggers etc.' Another soldier of the same period, Bellew, wrote an interesting comparison between British and Indian troops in his book *Memoirs of a Griffin*, published in 1843:

> Our countryman, the British soldier, possesses an unrivalled energy and bulldog courage which certainly, when the tug-of-war comes must, as it ever has done, bear all before it. But justice demands the admission that the sepoy contrasts most favourably with him – temperate, respectful, patient, subordinate and faithful – one of his highest principles being fidelity to his salt, to which he adds no ordinary degree of courage and every other requisite of a good soldier.

But Bellew stresses the importance of good relationships, of not taking, as most of the British did, the sepoy for granted:

The Saphead, Multan, a watercolour by J. B. Bellasis, who took part in the siege of Multan, 1848-9.

Details from *Bengal Troops on the March*, a panoramic sketch (nine metres long) made by an army officer, 1845.

We may bind them to us by the double link of affection and interest, if we study their feelings – but if inexperienced innovators trifle with their customs, we may find that they shake us off, like dew-drops from the lion's mane.

'Inexperienced innovators' did in the end help to bring about the Mutiny: reforms were introduced which infringed caste too deeply and showed a lack of understanding of the sepoy. But when the storm burst it was not in real terms a very big one; atrocities occurred and were given enormous publicity, though the British kept quiet about the equally nasty things that were done to Indians in reciprocation; fighting was mainly in Oudh, in the area between Allahabad, Lucknow and Delhi. It was only the Bengal Army which rebelled; the other

two Presidency Armies stood firm. W. H. Russell, the intrepid *Times* correspondent who reported from the front during the last part of the Mutiny, was very close to events and in the confidence of the British generals; yet even in the thick of battle he sees both sides and remarks on the continuing loyalty of sepoys. This is his entry in his *Indian Mutiny Diary* for 9 May 1858, beginning with a typical Victorian exaggeration:

> Assuredly, never was the strength and courage of any race tried more severely in any one year since the world began than was the mettle of the British in India in 1857. And yet, it must be admitted that, with all their courage, they would have been quite exterminated if the natives had been all and altogether hostile to them! The desperate defences made by garrisons were, no doubt, heroic; but natives shared the glory, and by their aid and presence rendered the defence possible. . . . Look at us all here in camp at this moment! Our outposts are native troops – natives are cutting grass for and grooming our horses, feeding the elephants, managing the transport, supplying the commissariat which feeds us, cooking our soldiers' food, cleaning their camp, pitching and carrying their tents, waiting on our officers, and even lending us money. . . . We never hear any public acknowledgment of their services.

But in general British reaction in India and at home in England was extreme and beyond reason: 'My blood courses like boiling lava through my veins as I write. . . . The swarthy demons of India must give account to the God whom they have insulted and defiled,' wrote an apoplectic military officer. Possibly reactions were so violent because the British knew that they depended on the sepoy for their security; suddenly the fidelity which they had taken so much for granted was in question. It was most unpleasant.

Yet things went back to normal fairly quickly; the civil administration, efficient and secure, continued as before. The crown took over the Company's Army; in 1861 it became part of the British Army. Closer attention was paid to class and caste in recruiting. More British soldiers were sent out; the numbers of Indians were reduced so that the proportions became one British to two Indian. But most thinking Victorians realized that, however powerful and well-organized the military might, no army of 200,000 men could hold an Empire of 300 million unless most of the ordinary people acquiesced in the government's rule. If the *ryots* of India had joined in the Mutiny, the British would have been wiped out and the Empire destroyed. It was not the power of the Army that held the Raj together, despite glib sayings like:

> *Whatever happens, we have got*
> *The Maxim gun, which they have not.*

It was a caring and efficient civil administration, which, with all its faults and ideological excesses, had India's interests at heart.

5 Social Life

English society in India did its best from the eighteenth century onwards to be a faithful replica of society at home, but it could never fully succeed: there were differences, strangenesses, exaggerations which tell us more about the nature of British-Indian society than the likenesses do. 'India is the paradise of middle-aged gentlemen,' pronounced a lady writing home from Madras in 1837; this was because young men in India 'are thought nothing of', being posted into remote areas to make or mar their fortunes; but 'at forty, when they are "high in the service", rather yellow, and somewhat grey, they begin to be taken notice of, and called "young men".'

This writer, who later published her letters anonymously, goes on to describe the *longueurs* of Madras dinner parties where the real young men sit silently by while the yellow and grey gentlemen 'do all the flirtation in a solemn sort of way'.

> The company are generally tired out with the heat and the office-work all day before they assemble at seven o'clock, and the houses are greatly infested by musquitoes, which are in themselves enough to lower one's spirit and stop conversation. People talk a little in a very low voice to those next to them, but one scarcely ever hears any topic of general interest started except steam navigation. . . . After dinner the company all sit round in the middle of the great gallery-like rooms, talk in whispers, and scratch their musquito-bites. Sometimes there is a little music, as languid as anything else. Concerning the company themselves, the ladies are all young and wizen, and the gentlemen are all old and wizen.

The writer was constantly surprised and appalled by the languid lethargy of the English women she met and their lack of interest in their surroundings.

> I asked one lady what she had seen of the country and the natives since she had been in India. 'Oh nothing!', said she: 'thank goodness, I know nothing about them, nor I don't wish to: really I think the less one sees and knows of them the better!'

The writer is determined to fight off this negative attitude and declares:

> this makes me wish to try and see everything that I can while the bloom of my Orientalism is fresh upon me, and before this apathy and listlessness have laid hold on me, as no doubt they will.

With the intelligence and energy she obviously had, she probably remained a person who enjoyed rather than suffered India.

Woodcut by a Sikh artist of a European couple seated at a table, the lady 'playing' a violin and the gentleman pouring wine. Their costumes are in the style of about 1825.

Pedlars of the Sudra Class, an illustration from *European Manners in Bengal* by Mrs S. C. Belnos, 1832. Mrs Belnos writes that: 'The heat of the climate being too intense to allow European customers to visit their shops so frequently as they would desire they fit up boxes with small drawers, with a variety of articles useful as well as ornamental, such as jewels real and artificial, English and French satins and silks, ribbons, muslins, cambric etc. all of which are bought from these hawkers considerably cheaper than at the shops.

'Here the lady is making the pedlar give the Ayah her cut, a customary fee which was always paid and gave annoyance to merchants and purchasers alike.'

Painting by an anonymous Calcutta artist, *c.* 1782, of Lady Impey in her boudoir. The Impeys were in India from 1774 to 1783. Sir Elijah served as Chief Justice of Bengal in the New Supreme Court. This domestic scene shows the servants spinning, sewing and embroidering. The gardener has brought in fruit and vegetables for Lady Impey's approval; her secretary ushers forward a tradesman with a bill. The milliner who is offering Lady Impey a new hat has a needle stuck in his turban. Sir Elijah's silver stick bearers are on duty, and a boy fans Lady Impey. *Punkahs* came into use between 1780 and 1785, but clearly the Impey household did not have them.

Englishwomen of the eighteenth and nineteenth centuries became lethargic and languid because of many reasons which did not apply in England: in India they had so many servants that they were expected to do nothing. With no useful role to play the heat affected them in a way it did not affect the men, who had to carry on regardless; frequent pregnancies and lack of proper medical care did not help. They were in a sense interlopers in a man's world and seemed to have reacted by setting exaggerated store on the maintaining of a tightly-knit artificial society as similar as possible to life in England. Unfortunate masculine habits like keeping native mistresses were frowned on until they eventually died out. The Reverend James Long, writing in the 1850s of an earlier Calcutta, quotes the story of

> an elderly military character, who solaced himself with no less than sixteen of all sorts and sizes! Being interrogated by a friend as to what he did with such a number: O! replied he, I give them a little rice, and let them run about. This same gentleman was paying his addresses to an elegant young woman lately arrived from Europe,

but who was informed by the lady at whose house she was residing of the state of affairs; the description closed with 'Pray, my dear, how would you like to share a sixteenth of a Major?'

The major, unrepentant, reckoned that the expenses of his mistresses were much less than those 'laid out upon some British damsels'.

The British might condemn oriental habits, like the keeping of *zenanas* (harems), but they could never get away from the fact that they were in the orient: behind their English social whirl was the strangeness of India and Indian servants, the heat, the pests, the long siestas, the swinging *punkahs* pulled by a native figure out on the verandah; the sounds of bazaar and temple away beyond the shuttered windows . . . . The tension between their English way of life and the oriental background was always there. Everything was strange to the newly-arrived Englishman, even if his compatriots had done their best to create the illusion of ordinary society when they met together.

'ainting by an anonymous Calcutta ırtist, *c.* 1782, of the Impey children vith their *ayahs* in the nursery of their Calcutta home. The cage-like mosquito ıets on the cots, the slatted blinds and he bowls of water under the cot-legs vere mentioned by Twining in his ontemporary description.

Interior of a house at Madura, Madras, in the 1860s.

Twining, arriving in Madras at the end of the eighteenth century, catches this impression of strangeness in his detailed account of his first night in Madras:

Here then [at the house of Mr Thomas Oakes on his first arrival at Madras] I slept, and had the first specimen of the luxurious or effeminate ways of an Indian life, some of the servants who were ordered to attend upon me laying hold of my sleeves to pull off my coat, while others unbuttoned my knees and in spite of all resistance began to pull off my stockings; when others brought a large bright brass vessel and washed my feet, pouring cold water upon them from black porous jars. The room was very lofty. The floor was covered with a fine mat, the walls with a fine shining plaster, without any ornament of pictures or glasses. The furniture was extremely simple, the chairs and sofa having merely cane bottoms, without cushions or covering of any kind, nor were there curtains to the spacious lofty windows, which moreover were not glazed, but consisted of movable green blinds, opening as folding doors from top to bottom. This simplicity which I observed in all the houses was not with any view to economy, for there was no appearance of *that*, but was suited to the climate, promoting coolness and preventing the accumulation of dust and insects, of mosquitoes particularly, of which I this first evening began to feel the tormenting annoyance, and lizards, of which I saw several running up and down the smooth walls of my chamber with extraordinary swiftness. I watched their motions as my attendants undressed me, but as they did not notice them, or looked at them with unconcern, I concluded they were harmless. . . .

My bed partook of the general simplicity and convenience and suitableness to the climate. It consisted of a hard mattress, covered with a sheet, and another folded at the bottom, that I might draw it over me if I pleased. It stood in four small vessels

Illustration of dancing boys from *European Manners in Bengal* by Mrs S. C. Belnos, 1832. She comments that 'they are not so expensive as a set of Hindoostan dancing girls, their movements are more animated than those of the other, their infantine voices are often shrill and disagreeable.'

Tom Raw Between Smoke and Fire. The illustration shows Tom Raw the Griffin at a lively dinner party, sitting next to the gentleman in white who appears to be in trouble with his *hookah*.

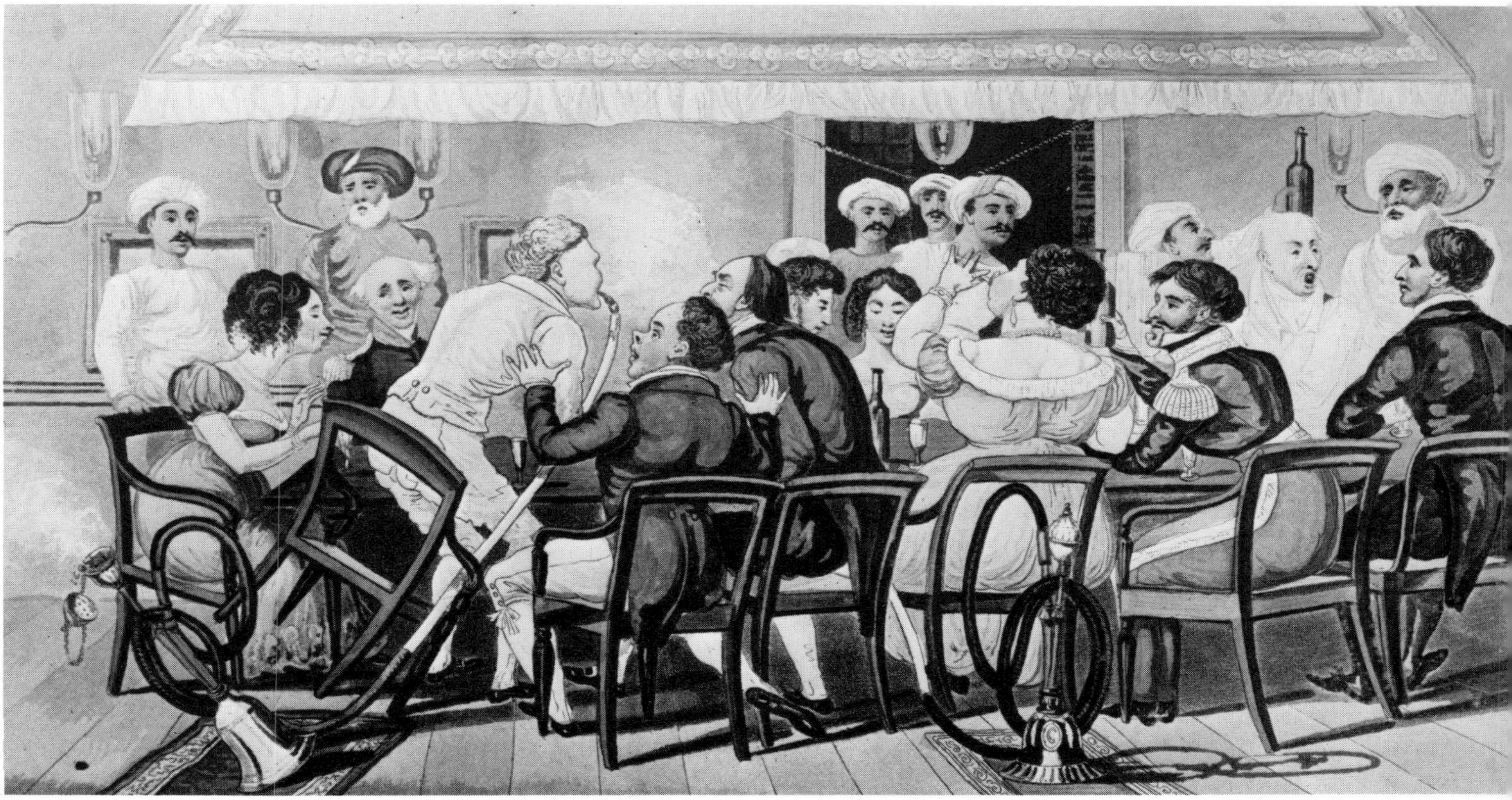

A Snake charmer, Exhibiting Snakes before Europeans, an illustration dating from 1813.

A Rajput drawing, *c.* 1820, of an English family at home. The scene depicts a serious domestic crisis, such as the announcement of bankruptcy and ruin. The dark hair of the wife suggests Eurasian blood; this is probably therefore a mixed marriage.

of water, that ants and other insects might not crawl up the posts, and was surrounded by mosquito curtains, or rather by *one* curtain which encircled it all round, for there was no opening at the sides, two men lifting it up at the bottom to let me in, flapping their cloths at the same time to drive away the mosquitoes, and putting it down quickly as soon as I had crept into my cage. As the weather was too hot for me to make use of the upper sheet, I found the convenience of the light drawers, and slept, as indeed was the general custom, in a similar dress ever afterwards.

Balls and routs, dinner parties and picnics, all took place in a setting so unlike England that perhaps this fact in itself caused the British to be exaggeratedly 'British' in their pursuit of pleasure. There was a feverish quality about their social life, particularly in the eighteenth century, which grew from basic uneasiness. This unease was caused by the alien country in which they all lived and, even more important, by the fact that the majority of the British in India were middle-class people living like aristocrats. Their way of life, with dozens of servants, large houses, ample leisure and sporting pastimes, was aristocratic; but they themselves came from middle-class backgrounds. Just to be British and a Company servant gave you *entrée* into society in the Presidencies: you were immediately part of a rigid social structure, and unless you were aristocratic or eccentric or both it was unlikely that you would have the courage or aplomb to disregard that structure and strike out for yourself. The pace was set and everyone observed it, with a resulting lack of spontaneity or relaxation. One often gets the impression from eighteenth- and nineteenth-century journals and letters of people trying hard to be what they are not. Emily Eden, with her sophisticated aristocratic background, says of a typical Calcutta party:

After dinner all the ladies sit in a complete circle round the room, and the gentlemen stand at the farther end of it. I do not suppose they would have anything to say if they met, but it would look better. Luckily it does not last long.

Surely these people she fixes with her critical eye have the stiffness of social insecurity.

Right from the start, when the East India Company decided that it would not 'employ any gentleman in any place of charge' but stick to traders and merchants, India was a place where an Englishman of humbler origin had an opportunity for social advancement which he would probably not have had in England. No man is more snobbish and keen on convention than the social climber; snobbery and convention were always part of British life in India. Even so, the number of English people in any place was usually so small that they had to stick together; class barriers between the English themselves had to come down or they would have had no one to talk to. Aristocrats employed by the Company after it had overcome its earlier prejudice against them (believing that good business and upper-class frivolity did not go together) had to mix socially with Englishmen they would never have got to know at all in England herself. There was a levelling-up as well as a levelling-down; and society itself, rigidly upper-class in structure, was very mixed in essence. Hence the unease

Victorian villa. It could be in England, except for the flat dust around it and the servants' *godowns* crouching behind on the right.

Watercolour by J. B. Bellasis entitled *European House and Garden*. This is a typical example of the album drawings made by English residents.

and lack of *savoire-faire* in the big Government House gatherings, described as 'such frosts' by Emily Eden and others like her. Lady Falkland wrote in 1868 from Bombay:

The ladies of Bombay are more tenacious of their rank than we are in England. . . . I once saw a lady, far from well, after a dinner party at Government House, and wishing very much to go home; who, on my urging her to do so, hesitated, because another person in the company – the wife of a man of higher official rank than her own husband – did not seem disposed to move. I took the opportunity of impressing upon the poor sufferer, that the sooner this custom was broken through, the better. However, she did not like to infringe it, and so she sat on.

One must not forget, though, that Victorian society back in England could be pretty stultified and stratified also.

During their time in India, the British relied mainly upon food, drink, all kinds of sport and, in the last hundred years, hill stations for their fun and relaxation. The practice of sport developed and widened during their time there but did not radically change; hill stations flowered immediately as a blessed release from the plains and then remained their static charming selves. The great changes, reflecting basic shifts of attitude and social habits, came in the consumption of food and, particularly, of drink.

In the early Settlement days the men were cooped up in their college-like factories, hemmed in by rules and regulations, pomp and ceremony, and they found the main outlet for their tension, apart from some sport and gambling,

William Hickey (1749?-1830). His *Memoirs* give an entertaining account of his life in India and other parts of the world, of his chequered career as an attorney and journalist, and of his fondness for women and claret. (Hickey is the seated figure.)

The communal bath, where the men on the station went in the morning after their rides to swim, be shaved and try to learn the knack of riding a *mussock*, a water-carrier's bag made from an inflated sheep-hide. *Mussocks* were also used for crossing rivers.

(Below) H. C. Tucker's plan of his house in India, *c.* 1833. His key to the plan is as follows:

- A Pucka godowns [Pucka = brick, as against mud or thatch servants' huts]
- B Wood store
- C Place where bearers boil the water
- D Verandah for palkees etc.
- E Bathing rooms
- G 4 Dressing rooms
- H Double enclosed verandah on *west*
- J Rooms for the pantry and Bearers.

(Tucker interestingly calls the courtyard which his wife and children use the 'Court for the Zenanah'.)

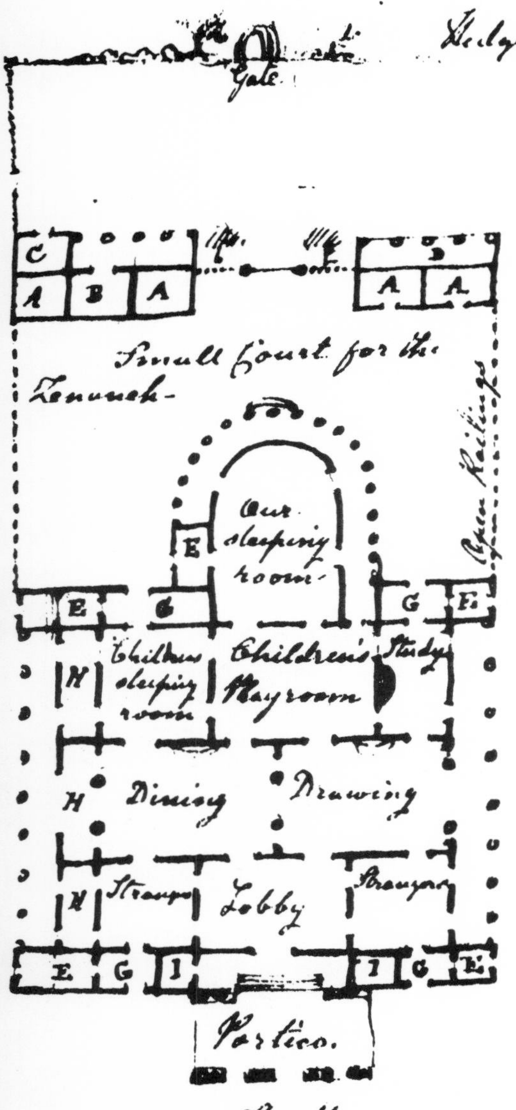

in alcohol. A Chaplain at Fort St George in 1676 wrote complaining bitterly to the Court of Directors in London of

> some of the Writers who by their lives are not a little scandalous . . ., so sinful in their drunkenness, that some of them play at cards and dice for wine that they may drink. . . . Others pride themselves in making others drink till they be insensible, and then strip them naked and in that posture (horresco referens) cause them to be carried through the streets to their dwelling place. Some of them, with other persons whom they invited, once went abroad to a garden not far off, and there continued a whole day and night drinking most excessively. . . . A person worthy of credit having occasion to go the next day into the same garden could number by the heads 36 bottles . . . it is their frequent custom to break bottles as soon as they have drunk the wine, and this they have done sometimes within the walls of the Fort, and withal, sing and carouse at very unseasonable hours.

The Company Directors had tried to enforce the rules that 'Whosoever shall appeare to be drunke shall pay five shillings for the use of the poore for every such offence. . . . And in defect . . . the offender shall sett in the stocks six houres.' All to no avail: Englishmen who worked in India then needed alcohol in large amounts to offset the tedium of life in a society of very limited numbers, and anyway until the nineteenth century all Englishmen drank more heavily than they did later. William Hickey, a famous Calcutta literary hack in the eighteenth century, describes in his diary 'the daily super-abundant potations of champagne and madeira'. He records how fourteen people consumed in one bout three and a half dozen bottles of claret and 'a proportionable quantity of Madeira'; it all ended with the glasses and candleshades being broken, 'pranks which too frequently finish drinking parties in this quarter of the globe'.

With the coming of large numbers of Englishwomen to India, with the growing popularity of dancing at social events which demanded that men stayed

(Left) *Mr Boulderson's House at Goruckpore*, a pencil and wash drawing by H. C. Tucker, 1833. H. C. Tucker owned this house in 1833 and sent an enthusiastic letter home to England describing the house in detail. He ends his letter: 'We have never in our lives been so well lodged, or had so well contrived a house, grounds, and out-offices. My study is rather small, but very cozy. It is our snuggery, and has both couch and fire – with a fine heavy punkah which I am making. May God make us grateful for these and all our other blessings – we have indeed many – My drawing in Mother's book is very like the place, and not embellished.'

perpendicular throughout the evening, and with the cold winds of the reformers blowing through society, excessive drinking waned. (The criticisms of society in *Letters from Madras*, written between 1836 and 1838, do not include inebriation.) In earlier days even women consumed large quantities of wine; one eighteenth-century woman wrote of family expenditure that 'Wine is the heaviest family article; for, whether it is taken favourably or medicinally, every lady even to your humble servant, drinks at least a bottle per diem, and the gentlemen four times that quantity.' 'Medicinally' is a reference to the fact that eighteenth-century doctors believed that wine, and port particularly, guarded you against fever in hot weather if you consumed enough of it. No wonder that there was a contemporary saying that 'Two monsoons are the age of a man.' English eating and drinking habits were the main reason why the death rate was so staggeringly high; as the Reverend Long said, 'with tables groaning under the weight of heavy joints of meat, washed down with Arrack-punch, it is not surprising that one third of the cases in hospital arose from liver-complaint.' One also suspects that doctors killed off as many people as over-indulgence did. Luckily for the survival of the English, eating and drinking habits became more sensible as the nineteenth century progressed.

By the end of the eighteenth century, the three Presidencies had acquired distinctive atmospheres: Bombay was regarded as very much a backwater (Bombay's great days were to begin with the opening of the Suez Canal in 1869); Madras had its high military population which gave a distinct flavour to its social life; and Calcutta was famous for its fevered cosmopolitanism. Calcutta was the base of the Governor-General, and Lord Wellesley's aristocratic grandeur made the city's society renowned.

The young Charles Metcalfe, arriving in Calcutta in 1801, while Wellesley was Governor-General, records his engagements in his diary. He was well connected, but even so the whirl of events is impressive. He has only just arrived from England:

Drawing by Captain Robert Smith of an early bungalow. The gentleman seated outside is smoking his *hookah* attended by a *hookah-burdar* and being fanned.

Some Indian Servants, a sketch made in 1896. They include the *chaprassi* (messenger) who is coming up to the horse with a letter; the *syce* (groom); the *derzi* (tailor); the *ayah*; the *khitmagar* (butler or head servant); the *mali* (gardener), who is holding a vegetable for the *khansama* (cook), and on the right the *bheestie* (water-carrier).

1801

Tues. 6 Jan. Went with Plowden to see Miss Baillie at Barlow's. Received an answer from Crommelin. Dined at home.

7 Jan. Went with Plowden to Brooke's. Saw Golding. Dined at Thornhill's. Got a Dhobee [launderer].

9 Jan. With Plowden in the morning. Was introduced to Sir Alured Clarke and General Baynard. Dined with the Governor-General who talked much about Eton. Went to Lady Anstruther's ball.

10 Jan. Shopping in the morning. Got a cocked hat (20 rupees). Dined and passing the evening at Dr. Dick's.

Sunday, 11 Jan. Called on Mr. Bazett. Dined with them.

12 Jan. Strolling about in the morning. Went to the levee. Dined at home and passed the evening at Colvin's.

13 Jan. Dined at College. Went to the Governor's ball.

14 Jan. Dined at Sir Alured Clarke's. At Dick's in the evening.

15 Jan. Dined at Mr. Graham's. Went to Brooke's ball. Sat up till sunrise at a second supper.

16 Jan. Dined at Tucker's. Went to bed very much fatigued, not having slept the previous night.

17 Jan. Dined at College. Sat at Higginson's. Had a Moonshee [native language teacher].

Sunday, 18 Jan. Dined at home. Had a Moonshee.

19 Jan. Dismissed my Moonshee, finding him of no use. Determined to teach myself.

Toy Puppet-show for English children, 1813.

The College he mentions is Fort William College, where Carey was teaching; it had just been founded.

The social round in which everyone indulged to varying extents in all three Presidencies could only be made possible by the plethora of servants possessed by every English family. In England, only the aristocracy had so many; in India, everybody had a great number because it was expected of them. Though the numbers had dropped by the end of the nineteenth century, there were still large numbers of servants per family; ten or more was quite normal during the twentieth century. The lady of the *Madras Letters*, who lived up-country and in no special magnificence, had twenty-seven. She writes wittily:

> Every horse has a man and a maid to himself – the maid cuts the grass for him; and every dog has a boy. I inquired whether the cat had any servants, but found she was allowed to wait upon herself; and as she seemed the only person in the establishment capable of so doing, I respected her accordingly.

Indefatigable Fanny Parkes, who travelled about India and wrote a book covering the years 1822 to 1844 called *Wanderings of a Pilgrim in Search of the Picturesque*, found that she and her husband 'as quiet people' needed fifty-seven, including a *dhobi*, *darzi* (tailor), cowherd, shepherd, poultryman and two carpenters. William Hickey (not a quiet person) had sixty-three. That some families had more is implied by Macrabie's exclamation in his *Journal* (1774-6), 'One hundred and ten servants to wait upon a Family of 4 People. Oh monstrous!' Only rich merchants, nabobs, could afford more than a hundred; these servants would include a dozen whose only duty was to wait at table; several cooks and bakers; many grooms, coachmen, *palanquin*-bearers; servants specially to look after the dogs; hairdressers, wig-barbers, several valets; maids for the ladies and *ayahs* for the children; launderers, gardeners, carpenters, and finally the *hookahburdar*, the man who looked after the gentleman's *hookahs* until the smoking of these went out of fashion in the nineteenth century.

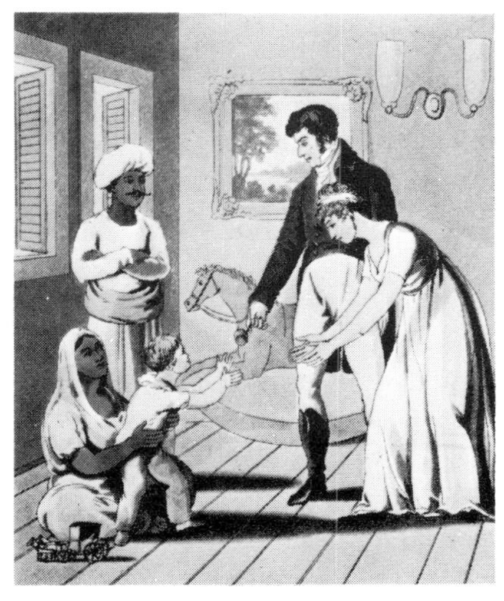

An English family with their *ayah*, 1813.

Civilians were not the only ones to have such large retinues; soldiers on campaign took their servants with them and the number they had was staggering. A captain in the Mysore Campaign of 1780 was accompanied by his steward, his cook, his valet, a groom and a groom's assistant, a barber, a washerwoman and 'other officers', besides fifteen coolies to carry his luggage, his wine and brandy, his live poultry and milch goats. These servants would often have their families with them – no wonder armies were such cumbrous things.

It is worth recording that many Englishmen rebelled against having these retinues of servants but discovered that the Indians themselves had constructed the system and did not approve of cutting down numbers: they needed these jobs and the places to live which went with them. Macrabie, who was a contemporary of Warren Hastings, writes angrily of

> The cursed examples of parade and extravagance they are holding up for ever to us. 'Master must have this. Master must do that.' A councillor never appears in the street with a train of less than twenty fellows, nor walks from one room to another in his house, unless preceded by four silver staves. . . . What improvement India may make in my affairs I know not, but it has already ruined my temper.

Bungalow in Simla in the late nineteenth century.

Lord Minto, Governor-General from 1807 to 1813, complained wryly that

> The first night I went to bed in Calcutta I was followed by fourteen persons in white muslin gowns into the dressing-room. One might have hoped that some of these were ladies; but on finding that there were as many turbans and black beards as gowns, I was very desirous that these bearded house-maids should leave me . . . which with some trouble and perseverance I accomplished and in that one room I enjoy a degree of privacy, but far from perfect.

Those British used to flocks of servants already or level-headed enough not to be too impressed by them were not affected by the grandeur of their large retinues. But many middle-class English people, women particularly, let their new status go to their heads and became insufferable, complaining in lordly tones of the 'niggers in the compound' and treating their servants badly. W. H. Russell describes two servants 'covered with plaisters and bandages, and bloody, who were lying on their charpoys [beds], groaning'. They had just been 'licked' by their employer: 'It is a savage, beastly and degrading custom,' said Russell, implying by the word custom that it happened fairly often. Servants were badly treated enough in England at the same period, but were even worse off in India. Modern eyes find it difficult to view the master/servant relationship objectively; but at least it is comforting to know that many English treated their Indian servants humanely and with greater kindness than the Mughals had before them, and that the millions of jobs for the Indians which the English provided during their Raj made economic sense.

The opening up of the hill stations in the nineteenth century made a dramatic difference to British life in India. It had taken them two hundred years to establish what the Mughals knew already: the delights of the Himalayan foot-hills. The Mughal Emperor and his court had escaped there when the heat of Delhi became unbearable. Jahangir loved Kashmir passionately and took his whole retinue every summer on the long journey to its beautiful lakes. Indians have a saying that no one who has seen Kashmir can be quite whole again, and it is fitting that Jahangir should have died on his way back from a long visit to his favourite place.

The English, military and civil alike, loved the hill stations, opening up roads to them as quickly as possible as the nineteenth century progressed. Even acid Emily Eden, who hated India so, was moved to say: 'Well, it really is worth all the trouble – such a beautiful place,' when she first arrived in Simla. Simla was the best known of the many northern hill stations because it became the seat of government in the hot weather. The whole Viceregal machine would move up there from Delhi, and the season would begin: endless balls, parties, pinics and amateur theatricals took place in a setting of incomparable beauty. Woodruff gives a vivid description of it.

St Stephen's Church, Ootacamund, Nilgiri Hills, a drawing done by George Hutchins Bellasis (1807-62), younger brother of J. B. Bellasis. He served in the Bombay Native Infantry and was sent on sick leave to Ootacamund in 1851, where this and many other sketches of Ooty were done.

Simla is the knot where half a dozen ridges of high ground meet, a starfish or an octopus of narrow ridges. There are roads along their crests; below the crests there are more roads, cut out from the hill-side before it gets too steep. Seen from the air, little roads wriggle and writhe like veins on a horse's neck. They are too narrow today for cars; they were always too narrow for carts or buggies. In Simla, you had to ride or walk or go in a rickshaw.

At intervals along these little roads would be a garden gate, from which a steep and winding path led to a bungalow. The path was often too steep for a rickshaw;

Sahibs and servants assembled for pig-sticking, Rampur, 1820.

on either side of it were usually little shelves where zinnias grew, blue lupins and many-coloured dahlias and everywhere, like a weed, pink cosmos. . . .

It was not at all like India . . . for everyone there was something a little fantastic about Simla. . . . It may have been the mixture of Surrey and Tibet, the perambulator on its way to the circulating library passing a slant-eyed woman with lumps of raw turquoise in her nose-ring, the baby slung like a tiny mummy on her back bumping against the wooden tube in which she mixed tea with salt and butter. Or it may have been the far vision of the snows, faintly reproachful alike of frivolity and toil.

The foothills of the Himalayas moved many people to say, with the Victorian Honoria Lawrence, 'while I live, I shall always be thankful that I have seen such beauty.' John Beames described a visit to a Buddhist monastery near Darjeeling with a sense of bated breath at the beauty of it all. He drinks tea with Tibetan monks:

It was brick tea, made of broken tea-leaves, stalks and refuse cemented into a cake with bullock's blood. It is made into a thick, soupy liquid, with hot water, salt, and rancid butter and, strange to say, is not nasty. When we emerged the monks had all disappeared and the great stone platform in front of the temple lay bare and white in the sunshine. All round was a view unparalleled in the whole world. Far below us the steep mountain slopes sank away through many gradations of colour, from rich, mellow green to deep greys and violets in the dark, sunless gorges. Across these narrow winding valleys rose other hills, and beyond them others, and yet others till, far off on the southern horizon, the eye dimly perceived Darjeeling on its wooded crescent with cloud-capped Senchal towering behind it. To the west the high shoulder of the hill shut out the view, but all along the northern sky stood in awful majesty the loftiest mountains in the world – a long white chain of snowy masses rifted into peaks and domes and ridges, none less than 25,000 feet in height. The shadowy clefts down their white flanks were deep purple and here and there a great glacier, like a waterfall suddenly frozen, hung arrested in the midst of its leap from a grey scarred peak. From the cloudy top of Kahsuperi, itself some 7,000 feet high, the eye

Tom Raw pig-sticking, 1828.

wandered down and up over peak after peak till stopped by the mighty wall of iron-grey rock streaked and lined with snow which reared up and up till it culminated in the triple top of Kanchangjinga. It was a sight such as one only sees once in a lifetime. One feels as if hung in mid-air between heaven and earth. The unfathomable depths of the great purple gorges, the constantly varying play of light and shadow on the soaring pinnacles of everlasting snow, the plumy, waving woods of every hue made up a picture rare and never to be forgotten.

Another hill station, Queen of the South as Simla was Queen of the North, is Ootacamund, or Ooty. Ooty was 'discovered' and opened up in the early nineteenth century; it is over 7000 feet up in the famous Blue Hills, the Nilgiris, of South India, which rise out of the scorching table-land of Mysore and Madras, where the temperature often stands at 110 degrees or more for months on end. Ooty, always fresh and cool, even cold, was worth the long trek. Mollie Panter-Downes describes the journey in her book *Ooty Preserved*:

The British who toiled up through the dense malarial jungle to Ootacamund in the nineteenth century must have found the journey no joke. If you were young and vigorous, you rode. If you were older, or young and lazy, you could go by bullock cart or be carried in a palanquin. According to an early guidebook to the Nilgiris (or Neilgherries, in the original spelling), the bullock carts averaged four and a half to five miles an hour; the horses did five to six, but they tired more quickly. The bullock-cart traveller's luggage was put in the wagon, boards were laid across the valises, and his bedding was placed on the top. Reclining regally thereon, he was towed away, with stops for refreshment and rest at the dak bungalows. Or he could refresh himself, having taken the precaution of seeing to it, as the guidebook strongly

Gentlemen mounting their elephants in preparation for the hunt, 1836.

Plate entitled *Our Camp*, from William Rice's *Tiger Shooting in India*, 1857. One tiger is being skinned; another skin has already been pegged out.

recommends, that the sides of the bullock cart were fitted with pockets of coarse cloth into which could be stowed the wine, the beer, the brandy, the kettle, the sacred teapot, and the other vital necessities of Indian life. By whatever means the visitors came, they were soon in ecstasies of amazement and delight. The newly discovered Ootacamund was hailed with rapture as a miraculous giver of health, even of life itself.

'It was like passing through the valley of Death to Paradise!' said a twenty-year-old Victorian subaltern as he gazed at the soft rounded green hills. When Lord Lytton, Viceroy from 1876 to 1880, was staying in Government House in this 'paradise', he wrote ecstatically to his wife:

it far surpasses all that its most enthusiastic admirers and devoted lovers have said to us about it. The afternoon was rainy and the road muddy, but such beautiful *English* rain, such delicious *English* mud. Imagine Hertfordshire lanes, Devonshire downs, Westmoreland lakes, Scotch trout streams, and Lusitanian views!

An earlier Victorian traveller, Richard Burton, goes into raptures too:

> You luxuriated in the cool air. Your appetite improved. The mutton had a flavour which you did not recollect in India. . . . You praised the vegetables, and fell into ecstasy at the sight of peaches, apples, strawberries and raspberries, after years of plantains, guavas and sweet limes. You, who could scarcely walk a mile in the low country . . . wandered for hours over hill and dale without being fatigued. With what strange sensations of pleasure you threw yourself upon the soft turf bank and plucked the first daisy which you ever saw out of England! And how you enjoyed the untropical occupation of sitting over a fire in June!

Yet for all this Ooty was not quite like England: the climate still had a touch of savagery about it. The rounded green hills so reminiscent of home were cultivated by a strange aboriginal tribe called the Todas, unlike any other tribe in India. The thickets teemed with Indian game, the lakes with fish. Ooty was, to quote Panter-Downes again,

> an English dream made a shade delirious and out of true by the high, thin air, combined with all that many a heart loved with passion in India – the outdoor life, the horses, the wild animals, the early wakings in the Indian mornings, with their matchless dazzling purity that makes each day seem the first ever created.

The Victorians, enchanted with their discovery, developed Ooty, built little gabled cottages called Apple Cottage and Cheerful Cottage, turretted houses called Woodcote Hall and Grasmere Lodge. From the 1820s onwards Madras families built their summer houses, and by the 1870s the Governor of Madras and his whole secretariat moved up to Ooty for the hot weather. The men rode and fished and shot game which included tiger and wild boar; the Ootacamund Hunt was formed in 1844 and hunted jackals instead of foxes. There was tennis and golf; the Club and the Anglican Church; the gymkhanas and polo.

The Prince of Wales' first tiger, Jaipur, 1876.

The rolling green downs, the waterfalls, the giant trees which made shady walks for the women, the luxuriant English flowers and vegetables: all this was indeed paradise for the English escaped from the hot plains.

The Victorian Englishman believed in the virtue of strenuous exertion, in both work and play. Activity became virtually an end in itself: 'To recommend contemplation in preference to action is like preferring sleeping to waking,' said Sir Leslie Stephen. English diversions from work were masculine and energetic: polo, big game hunting, pig-sticking. Activities like these were thought to have as important an effect on character as work did: they produced that much-admired quality, manliness – the tough upper lip, the physical perseverance, the ability to lead and organize others. (This often went hand in hand with a contempt for intellectual or aesthetic pursuits; when a young Victorian civil servant took a piano out to his district, it was regarded by an eminent contemporary, John Lawrence, as an unpardonable offence: 'I'll smash his piano for him,' he said.)

Polo and pig-sticking, those very Anglo-Indian pursuits, were ideal 'manly' activities needing strength, toughness and quickwittedness. That vigorous sort of horse-borne hockey, polo, a game native to India, was played in all the larger stations by civilians, but it was most popular in the Indian Army. When Winston Churchill joined it fresh from Sandhurst he found that he and his companions 'devoted ourselves to the serious purpose of life. This was expressed in one word – Polo.' They played polo for hours on end, day after day. It kept them extremely fit and fully occupied during otherwise boring periods of garrison life. But pig-sticking, even more than polo, was regarded as 'the game of games' by all who practised it. It had the advantage for the lonely

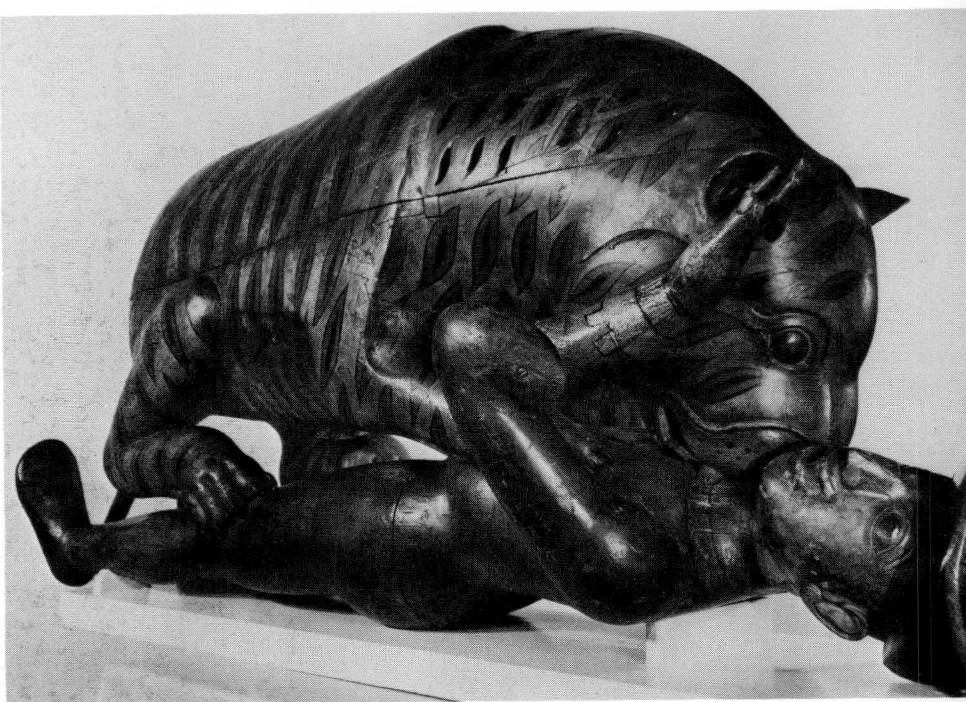

Tipu's Tiger, a carved wooden effigy containing a miniature organ, presented by the French to Tipu Sultan *c.* 1795.

Watercolour by J. B. Bellasis, entitled *Refreshing after Hard Day's Shooting*.

district officer of being something he could do on his own or in small groups. In a life of heavy responsibility and much loneliness, it was the hard physical exertions of things like pig-sticking which preserved civilians' sanity and sense of proportion.

Philip Woodruff, often quoted in this book, served as a district officer in India and was himself a devotee of pig-sticking. He points out that anyone pig-sticking had to be an excellent horseman, to have 'a power of quick and cool judgment, a stout heart, a controlled but fiery ardour and a determination not to be beaten', and that these same qualities were also needed for a good district officer. Here is his description of pig-sticking:

> The civilian, but hardly anyone else, often hunted pig alone. And to kill a pig with a spear by oneself is an achievement. A boar can go faster than a horse for three or four hundred yards; a man must drive in his heels and gallop as hard as he can to keep the beast in sight. This first gallop, at a pace unknown to fox-hunters, was always through thick country with long grass or tamarisk bushes and usually cut up by water-courses. After that first burst, if his horse still knows where the boar is, the hunter must use judgment, hustling it perhaps at a hard gallop through the broken country but not pressing too close among the tamarisk, going as hard as he can the moment an open patch is seen, trying all the time to tire the pig, so that he can catch it when he sees it clearly, or so that it will turn at bay. When it does turn to fight – and the bigger the boar the sooner that will be – he may advance at a walk relying on straight eye, strong arm and keen spear to keep the sharp tusks from his horse's legs and his own, or he may meet its charge at the gallop, or perhaps spear the defiant beast as he gallops past.

Deer Hunting, a plate from Sir Charles D'Oyly's *Lithograph Scrapbook*. Sir Charles D'Oyly (7th baronet, 1781-1845) went to India in 1797. He was Opium Agent in Patna from 1821 to 1831, then Resident until 1833, then Customs Officer until 1838. He was a prolific artist. Many Europeans stopped at Patna in order to meet him and see his work. He imported and ran a lithographic press with the help of local Indian artists, whom he greatly influenced. He formed a local art society 'for the promotion of Arts and Sciences, and for the circulation of fun and merriment of all descriptions'.

Though not so physically arduous as pig-sticking, tiger-hunting had its excitements and dangers. Tiger hunts could be grand affairs, but often they were expeditions carried out at the demand of villagers who were losing cattle. G. F. Atkinson, in his light-hearted but cruel book about a station in India in the 1840s, *Curry and Rice on Forty Plates*, published in 1859, describes 'Our Tiger-Shooting':

This morning an aggrieved agriculturist came howling into the cantonments, reporting the sudden apparition of a tiger, only fifteen miles off, which had abstracted his oxen and his fatlings, and evinced a desire, moreover, to elope with his wife.

Atkinson and his party decide to hunt it next morning:

But the morning gun has fired; our valet has roused us from our hard cot and our soft slumbers; we have quaffed our Bohea, mounted our Arabs, and galloped to the

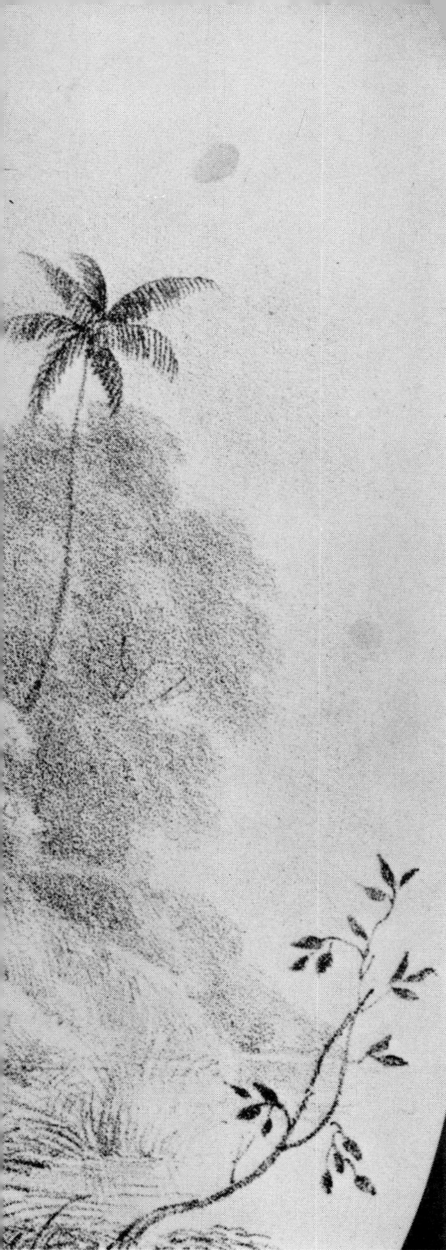

scene of action. The elephants are all prepared, with their sporting howdahs duly stocked with their batteries. The afflicted agriculturist is there, and points out with looks of anguish 'the vestiges of (the tiger's) creation', in the shape of the bones of his favoured bullock, which the famished tiger then and there devoured, as we see some watery-mouthed schoolboy devouring at the pastrycook's door the tartlets he had thought to carry home, but which hunger and a wistful eye could not resist. We listen to his tale of woe, hear that two more bullocks have been abstracted, and we promise the full value of all, and of many more, if he will but show us the tiger.

Away then we start. With cunning eye the beaters track the foot-prints in the shade. He has got into the jungle, and now the track is lost; the beaters form in line. Away we go; we strain our eyes in every direction; occasionally we have a false alarm, then the elephants turn up their trunks, and go trumpeting along, crushing down the jungle – at times into the deep ravines, into which they lower their huge bodies so carefully and so well, then clambering up again, press onward on their way. A beater gives a shout – he is on the track – he sees blood upon the trampled grass. The sun has begun to beat down its penetrating rays upon our turbaned heads, which need the still greater protection of the umbrella. Another shout! A yell, followed by a roar from the tiger, and two sharp cracks from a double rifle, announces to the field that the game has been found.

The tiger tries to escape, is headed off, attacks the tail of an elephant, and then is finally killed.

The victim is hoisted on to a pad elephant, we refresh ourselves with the necessary beverages, tramp back on our elephants to the rendezvous, mount our Arabs, and gallop back to cantonments in time for tiffin, delighted and properly baked in our morning's amusement, and long to hear of another tiger having ventured into the dangerous proximity of 'Our Station'.

The clumsy, jocular tone of this book is typical of Victorian writing about social life in India.

Large official tiger-hunts were quite different affairs, with dozens of elephants and *mahouts* and a big base camp. Often, to make a shooting camp run smoothly, the *mahouts* had to be given a regular supply of opium (*bhang*) to steady nerves and tempers. The use of bhang went further, as the Goddens point out in *Shiva's Pigeons*:

If an important guest is invited to shoot – in the old days it might have been the Viceroy . . . he must at least see if not shoot, a tiger. To make sure he does, the kill to which the tiger will return, and the drinking holes, may be doctored with opium. Tigers can become opium addicts.

Tigers have always held a fascination for the British: they are a magnificent part of wild India and a symbol of the dangerous side of Indians themselves. Tipu Sultan gave the British a great deal of unpleasant trouble during the Mysore Wars which culminated in his defeat in 1799, and 'Tipu' as everyone knew meant 'tiger' or 'conqueror of the woods'. The British have a constant reminder of Tipu's dislike of them in the splendid mechanical tiger now in the Victoria and Albert Museum. Not only is it in the process of furiously mauling an Englishman, but if it is wound up ghastly shrieks and murderous growls are emitted while the poor Englishman flaps one hand in vain. John Keats, who saw the tiger when it was on view in the East India Company's offices in

Duck Shooting from Sir Charles D'Oyly's *Lithograph Scrapbook*.

Leadenhall Street, describes ironically in his poem *The Cap and Bells* the noise which

> *Comes from a play-thing of the Emperor's choice,*
> *From a Man-Tiger-Organ, prettiest of his toys.*

Sport in India was always 'larger than life'; the animals bigger, the catches vast. Forbes, in his *Oriental Memoirs* of the years 1765 to 1783, describes a shoot which took place in Bengal:

A gentleman lately engaged on a shooting party in the wilds of Plassey, gave us an account of their success in one month, from August the 15th to September the 14th, in which space they killed one royal tiger, six wild buffaloes, one hundred and eighty-six hog-deer, twenty-five wild hogs, eleven antelopes, three foxes, thirty-five hares, one hundred and fifty brace of partridges and floricans, with quails, ducks, snipes, and smaller birds in abundance.

Such a large bag was not all that unusual; the *Oriental Sporting Magazine* for October 1829 gives

A List of Game killed by a Gentleman in the Neilgherries (Nilgiris) within the last six months.

Thirty three and a half couple of woodcock; 30 head of black deer . . .; 1 jungle sheep; 3 wild dogs; 7 bears; 7 hogs; 1 royal tiger, length 9 feet 7 inches; 1 cheeta; 100 brace and upward of jungle fowl and spur fowl; 20 brace and more of hares; 12 brace or more of peafowl; brace of quail, often 8 to 10 brace a day; snipe, 4 or 5 brace a day; imperial pigeon, 20 brace.

The royal tiger he dropped dead with one ball . . . 10 miles from Ootacamund. Such a list of killed and bagged may highly excite hopes of sporting visitors to these regions, but it must be borne in mind that such a staunch and indefatigable sportsman as Captain R. is rarely to be found.

It was a fortunate thing for the future of wild life in India that the excesses of Captain R. were the exception rather than the rule. It is not fair to blame him;

Hare Shooting from Sir Charles D'Oyly's *Lithograph Scrapbook.*

the manly ideal of the nineteenth century, with its emphasis on physical prowess, on being a good shot, a good rider and a good trencherman, hardly encouraged a sense of responsibility towards wild animals.

The manly ideal remained unquestioned until the First World War. The Empire at its height, the Victorian Raj, depended for its strength on the tacit acceptance of this manly ideal as the right way for an Englishman to behave both in work and play. The First World War destroyed this ideal, and with the arrival of doubt in all its manifestations the Raj weakened – or perhaps grew up: one can hold both views at once. After all, India is a country of complex contradictions where the single Hindi word *kal* means both yesterday and tomorrow.

Epilogue

> The British Power in India is like a vast bridge over which an enormous multitude of human beings are passing, and will (I trust) for ages to come continue to pass, from a dreary land, in which brute violence in its roughest form had worked its will for centuries – a land of cruel wars, ghastly superstitions, wasting plague, and famine – on their way to a country of which, not being a prophet, I will not try to draw a picture, but which is at least orderly, peaceful, and industrious, and which, for aught we know to the contrary, may be the cradle of changes comparable to those which have formed the imperishable legacy to mankind of the Roman Empire. The bridge was not built without desperate struggles and costly sacrifices. A mere handful of our countrymen guard the entrance to it and keep order among the crowd. If it should fall, woe to those who guard it, who to those who are on it, who to those who would lose with it all hopes of access to a better land. Strike away either of its piers and it will fall, and what are they? One of its piers is military power: the other is justice; by which I mean a firm and constant determination on the part of the English to promote impartially and by all lawful means, what they (the English) regard as the lasting good of the natives of India.

So wrote James Fitzjames Stephen, and, great Victorian political philosopher though he was, his imperialism falls ill on modern ears. The picture is rousing and idealistic without perhaps meaning to be; though containing its grain of truth, it grandiloquently overstresses the beneficence of British power. For Stephen and many like him, India was

> a country where we can govern and where we can work and make money and lead laborious lives; but which no Englishman ever did, or ever will, or can feel one tender or genial feeling. The work that is done here is great and wonderful; but the country is hateful.

Fortunately Stephen was wrong about the average Englishman in India: 'tender and genial' feelings were felt by many for India, and it was certainly not a hateful country to the majority. The British would not have flocked there for three hundred years if Stephen's words had been true. As usual there is a great divide between what the political theorists believed and what those who did the practical administration felt. John Beames gives us a closer impression of the real pleasures and difficulties of running an empire than does his contemporary Stephen. One needs the views of both to understand the phenomenon of the Raj, its rise and its apogee; and even then the picture is so complex that almost any general statement about British India is both true and false.

Portrait by Y. Wates of Sir James Fitzjames Stephen (1829-94) (Leslie Stephen's brother). He was legal member of the Governor-General's council in India from 1869 to 1872 and later a judge of the High Court (1879-91). He wrote a number of legal and political works.

Two more quotations will serve to illustrate very different and differing British attitudes towards their Raj. The first is expressed by the Reverend James Long in his book about Calcutta. His rosy view of the future as yet untainted by the Mutiny shows as clearly as anything could why the Indians were justified in their fears of British takeover:

The future opens out a bright scene – when Brahmanism will be in Bengal, as Buddhism is now, 'a thing of the past' – when Gospel light and its handmaid the English language and literature shall be diffused far and wide – when Municipal institutions, Colleges, Agricultural Societies and town Libraries shall have dispersed the terror of Mofussil life – when railroads intersecting the country shall have helped to scatter to the winds all local prejudices – and when the banks of the Bhagirathi [the river near Calcutta], like the banks of the Rhine or Thames, shall be ornamented with villas, country seats, and all the indications of a highly civilized state of society – when the upper classes of English Society in Calcutta – instead of being crowded together in their aristocratic mansions in Chowringi, the hot bed of Anglican prejudice and the focus of all those who cherish their irrational exclusiveness towards the natives of this land – shall enjoy the quiet and retirement of their dwellings along the course of the sacred stream, living thirty or fifty miles from Calcutta, but coming daily to it to do business through the wonderful facilities of travelling which will then be afforded.

This pious hope for a re-creation of Kingston-upon-Thames in Calcutta is so wide of the mark in every way that one has to make a real effort of the imagination to understand a man who wrote it from the heart. The Mutiny disposed of social and religious dreams like Long's, though India continued to have her woolly romantics.

The other extreme in British attitudes is expressed in his book *The India We Left* by Lord Trevelyan (great-nephew of Charles Edward Trevelyan), who served in India at the very end of the Raj. Pragmatic, realistic, unromantic, this attitude looked at the facts and got the work done:

We of the last generation served India to the best of our ability, without any missionary spirit or feeling of dedication or devotion to a cause. We served because it was our job and because we enjoyed it. Our Indian friends seemed to consider us sympathetic without being patronising. We had little use for Englishmen who ceased to be English and tried, from the best of motives, to become Indian in outlook and habits. We believed we could best serve our own country and India by remaining ourselves. When Indian and British interests conflicted, we took the view which we thought right for India. We were convinced that the British had brought great benefits to India, but, in the end, that it was time for us to leave. India was our life. That life was, in part, harsh and unattractive and cut us off from our own country, but it was, in the main, rewarding. We were content we had chosen it.

Romantics and realists, visionaries and pragmatists, theorists and grass-roots-wallahs, traders and statesmen: the British Raj was founded on them all.

Bibliography

MILDRED ARCHER *British Drawings in the India Office Library*, vols. I and II, London, 1969

MILDRED ARCHER *Company Drawings in the India Office Library*, London, 1972

MILDRED ARCHER *Natural History Drawings in the India Office Library*, London, 1962

W. G. and M. ARCHER, *Indian Painting for the British 1770-1880*, Oxford, 1955

GEORGE F. ATKINSON, *Curry and Rice on Forty Plates*, 2nd edition, London, 1859

PAT BARR, *The Memsahibs*, London, 1976

JOHN BEAMES, *Memoirs of a Bengal Civilian*, London, 1961

EDWARD BLUNT, *The I.C.S.*, London, 1937

HILTON BROWN (ed.), *The Sahibs – The Life and Ways of the British in India as Recorded by Themselves*, London, 1948

S. PEARCE CAREY, *Life of William Carey*, London, 1923

MICHAEL EDWARDES, *History of India*, London, 1961

WILLIAM FOSTER (ed.), *Early Travels in India*, London, 1921

WILLIAM FOSTER, *England's Quest for Eastern Trade*, London, 1963

HOLDEN FURBER, *John Company at Work*, Oxford, 1951

BAMBER GASCOIGNE, *The Great Moghuls*, London 1971

JON and RUMER GODDEN, *Shiva's Pigeons – An Experience of India*, London, 1972

PERCIVAL GRIFFITHS, *The British Impact on India*, London, 1952

PERCIVAL GRIFFITHS, *The British in India*, London, 1946

PERCIVAL GRIFFITHS, *A Licence to Trade*, London, 1972

FRANCIS HUTCHINS, *The Illusion of Permanence* (*British Imperialism in India*), Princeton, 1967

KENNETH INGHAM, *Reformers in India* (*1793-1833*), Cambridge, 1956

DENNIS KINCAID, *British Social Life in India* (*1608-1937*), London, 1958 and 1973

REVEREND JAMES LONG, *Calcutta and Its Neighbourhood*, Calcutta, 1974

PETER MARSHALL, *East Indian Fortunes* (*The British in Bengal in the 18th Century*), Oxford, 1976

PHILIP MASON, *A Matter of Honour – An Account of the British Army in India*, London, 1974

THOMAS METCALFE, *The Aftermath of Revolt 1857-1870*, Princeton, 1965
PAMELA NIGHTINGALE, *Trade and Empire in Western India*, London, 1970
MOLLIE PANTER-DOWNES, *Ooty Preserved*, London, 1967
W. H. RUSSELL (ed. Michael Edwardes), *My Indian Mutiny Diary*, London, 1957
PERCIVAL SPEAR, *India, A Modern History*, Michigan, 1961
PERCIVAL SPEAR, *Master of Bengal – an Illustrated Life of Clive*, London, 1975
PERCIVAL SPEAR, *The Nabobs – The Social Life of the English in 18th Century India*, London, 1932
ERIC STOKES, *English Utilitarians in India*, Oxford, 1959
HUMPHREY TREVELYAN, *The India We Left*, London, 1972
FRANCIS WATSON, *A Concise History of India*, London, 1974
PHILIP WOODRUFF, *The Men Who Ruled India*, vol. 1 *The Founders*, vol. 2 *The Guardians*, London, 1953 and 1954

Index

Page numbers printed in italic figures refer to illustrations